Female Subjectivity in Women's Writing

Female Subjectivity in Women's Writing

By

Hatice Yurttaş

Cambridge
Scholars
Publishing

Female Subjectivity in Women's Writing

By Hatice Yurttaş

This book first published 2023

Cambridge Scholars Publishing

Lady Stephenson Library, Newcastle upon Tyne, NE6 2PA, UK

British Library Cataloguing in Publication Data
A catalogue record for this book is available from the British Library

ISBN (10): 1-5275-2890-1
ISBN (13): 978-1-5275-2890-1

For Gülseren Yurttaş

TABLE OF CONTENTS

ACKNOWLEDGEMENTS

This book is based on my master's thesis that I wrote at Istanbul University in 2008. I would like to thank my supervisor Asst. Prof. Canan Şavkay for her help and kindness in writing this thesis at the English Language and Literature Department. I also wish to thank all the sister-mother-teacher-women who have entered my life for long or short, for good or bad so far for contributing to the 'I' of these sentences.

ABBREVIATIONS

Speculum: *Speculum of the Other Woman*
Thinking: Thinking the Difference for a Peaceful Revolution
The Way: The Way of Love
This Sex: This Sex Which Is Not One
An Ethics: An Ethich of Sexual Difference
NC: Nights at the Circus
BA: The Blind Assassin
ME: Morpho Eugenia

INTRODUCTION

The human subject has come to occupy a central role in recent literary criticism and this concern owes a lot to feminism which has initiated the awareness that the subject is not a natural, biologically determined, apolitical, or neutral entity but it is a socially constructed political being. Until the twentieth century, the subject was a trustworthy and dependable source of the knowledge of the world and itself. With the rise of psychoanalysis and deconstruction, it lost its position as the objective, self-conscious source of epistemology. Freud's conception of the subject under the control of unconscious drives and processes opens up a wide spectrum of views of how this subject comes to be. Lacan's fundamental contribution to the understanding of the subject with language as constitutive of its formation and initiation into society with a specific gender has attracted profound attention from feminist critics who embark on explaining how the individual comes to attain gender in hierarchical relations. Derrida's work on Western thought hinging on binary oppositions that create the illusion of a uniform, stable subject is closely linked to psychoanalysis' focus on the constitution of the subject.

Luce Irigaray is one of the important critics in this stream who provides a critical reading of these two approaches, namely Jacques Lacan's theory of the formation of the subject and Jacques Derrida's criticism of Western philosophy in order to analyse how gender is constructed in language and how the production of meaning is related to this construction. Inasmuch as theory is produced in language, Irigaray investigates how historical factors shape theory widening the scope of theory so as to discuss women's position in language, literature, philosophy, and in society. In this study, I will offer a reading of three postmodern works of fiction, whose writers have occupied a large space in postmodern theories and feminisms. I will read Angela Carter's *Nights at the Circus*, Margaret Atwood's *The Blind Assassin*, and A.S. Byatt's "Morpho Eugenia" in the light of Irigaray's criticism of patriarchy that focuses on the formation of subjectivity in language and theory. My aim is to analyse how these women writers respond and contribute to Irigaray's call for a language that can express sexual difference.

Angela Carter, Margaret Atwood, and A. S. Byatt's concern with the problem of representation and woman's position as a subject in literature manifests itself in the intertextuality and the choice of subject matter in their novels. It is not only that they choose women as main characters in these , but also and more significantly, the fact that they depict these characters as writers reflects their need to reassess, consider, negotiate, or change their position as women writers in literature. The intricate intertextuality that includes the frequent direct and indirect allusions to other works and placing inner texts contributed by different characters in the novels in *Nights at the Circus*, *The Blind Assassin*, and "Morpho Eugenia" demonstrates the woman writer's discomfort within genre boundaries. In *Female Stories, Female Bodies*, Lidia Curti argues that a link between genre and gender can be established in order to understand the particularity of intertextual writings of contemporary woman writers. She argues that women's struggle to transgress gender constraints have accompanied experiments with crossing genre boundaries as well. The attempt to reveal the artificiality and social construction of gender and the part genre plays in constructing gender in order to articulate sexual difference finds its expression in what she calls "genre contamination" (Curtie 1998, 48). The revisions of the literary canon and genres serve to give voice to women and female experience: "Genre is traversed by the discourse of sexual difference as if the vicinity of the two English words- genre and gender, divided by 'd' (for difference?)— recalled coincidence and dislocation, obedience and transgression at one and the same time" (Curtie 1998, 53). From this point of view, I will argue that the intertextuality in *Nights at the Circus*, *The Blind Assassin*, and "Morpho Eugenia" poses a critical stance towards both genre and gender construction in genre. By choosing a female protagonist in the picaresque structure in *Nights at the Circus*, Carter calls attention to the fact that in picaresque novels it is men who are the searching subjects -searching for women, knowledge, maturity, etc., and women are depicted either as the object of their search or their partners. Carter does not only make the female the searching subject in her novel, but she also designates female subjective identity as the object of the quest. As a *bildungsroman,* again, it is not the education of a man to fit into the social order with a marriage, but it is the education of woman in order to learn how woman is constructed in patriarchal order and how to survive in the male dominated society.

In *The Blind Assassin*, autobiographical writing helps Atwood reveal the fact that language has boundaries and these limits inhibit the representation of female identity and experience. Atwood also poses a bold challenge to the genre by altering the traditional endings of the novel which is marriage. Instead of marriage or *the union of lovers*, *The Blind Assassin* offers writing and producing an alternative identity in language for the ending of the novel. For example, she implies a different ending for *Pride and Prejudice*, which, as Bouson notes, is similar to *The Blind Assassin* with the two sisters and two suitors structure (Bouson 2003). Similarly, she offers divorce and a single life to Bertha Mason in *Jane Eyre* by presenting Iris who, like Bertha Mason, drinks and has sex outside the marriage institution, but who fights back and survives by writing whereas Bertha Mason is locked in the attic by her husband (Bronte 1994). While Bertha Mason never appears as the subject in *Jane Eyre*, Atwood frees woman from being defined as mad in male discourse by turning her into the subject of her own discourse and truth. With another allusion by choosing the name Aimee for a girl whose paternal ancestry is suspicious in *The Blind Assassin*, Atwood seems to send her compliments to Carter who states that "'father' is a hypothesis but 'mother' is a fact" alongside her warning to Daniel Defoe who deprives woman of her maternal heritage in *Roxana* (qtd. in Curti 1998, 103).

In "Morpho Eugenia" Byatt makes use of fairy-tale, *bildungsroman* and gothic genres but she disrupts the expectations from these genres. She employs fairy-tale structure for the purpose of giving voice to suppressed women like Matilda and Miss Mead, however, these voices are overshadowed by Adamson's search which dominates the female's, Matilda's search. Also, the woman or the woman writer subjects her desire to the male desire. In view of the fact that Matilda's writing serves to bring about enlightenment to Adamson's life in addition to her need for confirmation from Adamson, I will argue that in "Morpho Eugenia" male discourse prevails over woman's language.

As the intertextuality of *Nights at the Circus*, *The Blind Assassin*, and "Morpho Eugenia" indicates, Carter, Atwood, and Byatt deal with the problem of representation and female subjectivity. It is at the junction of female subjectivity and language in these writings that Irigaray's criticism of language as the source of gender construction becomes relevant to these writings. Before moving to the particularity of each work in their approach to language and gender, I would like to discuss Irigaray's critique of language and of patriarchal culture in the following part.

I. Psychoanalysis: Female subjectivity

Simon de Beauvoir's famous statement "One is not born woman but becomes a woman" in *The Second Sex* that was published in 1949 started an era in which the philosophy of subjectivity, language, and epistemology has had to confront the question of gender in view of the historical, cultural, sociological determinants linked to the structure of language and production of truth (Beauvoir 1993, 249). The second half of the twentieth century has witnessed a proliferation on theoretical debates on gender, which has reflected on literature since literature has become both the convict of representation as such and the domain of the prospect of producing a language that can disrupt the phallocentric gender representation. Irigaray's *Speculum of the Other Woman,* published in 1974 in French, has introduced a comprehensive reading of psychoanalytic theory and philosophy that demonstrates how language and the production of truth are determined by the male economy of desire. *Speculum* has contributed to debates on sexual difference especially after its translation into English by a strong argument on the significance of the mother-daughter relationship in the formation of female subjectivity and of the relation between desire and language.

Although Irigaray's theory is a critique of deconstruction and psychoanalysis, what she does is apply psychoanalysis and deconstruction on these theories, which means psychoanalyzing Lacan and deconstructing Derrida. Her reading aims to show that sexual difference which psychoanalysis attempts to explain determines psychoanalytic theory itself and deconstruction does not recognize sexual difference. For an understanding of Irigaray's argument for the need of a female subjective identity, a summary of her reading of Freud and Lacan is necessary first as she performs in the first section of *Speculum* titled "The Blind Spot of an Old Dream of Symmetry" and in *This Sex Which Is Not One*. I will discuss this before I turn to her criticism of deconstruction which is based on her criticism of psychoanalysis, especially on her attempt to introduce sexual difference into language and society as an alternative way to deconstruct the male-subject.

According to Freud, sexual difference, that is acquiring the position of man or woman occurs at the oedipal stage and before this stage, there is only one libido. In the anal stage, both the girl and the boy show the same aggressive impulses, and in the phallic stage, they continue to be theorized as little men; the boy has the penis and the girl has the clitoris as the equivalent of the penis for deriving sexual pleasure from. In masturbation, the vagina for sexual pleasure is not discovered and the clitoris is the only erogenous organ for the girl. The desire is for the phallic mother whom the baby wishes to get with a child. The differentiation of sexes occurs in the oedipal stage through the castration complex that is initiated by the sight of the opposite sex's genitals, but the effect of this sight works differently for the girl and the boy. Having seen the penis and deciding that it is better and bigger than her own inferior penis-clitoris, the girl ends up with acquiring penis-envy attributing the responsibility of her lack of the penis to her mother. Upon this recognition, the girl achieves womanhood by developing an antagonism towards her mother for not possessing one or not providing the girl with one, and this disappointment induces the girl into desiring her father in the hope that he may give her one and into an expectation that her clitoris may grow to be a penis one day. Hopefully, if she becomes a mother of a son in the future, she will substitute her child with the longed- for penis. For the boy, on the other hand, the sight of the vagina, the lack of a penis will work as a threat upon which he will terminate his masturbatory activities but not his desire for his mother because he will identify with the father and take a wife to substitute his desire for the mother in the future.

Lacan introduces the real, the imaginary, and the symbolic dimension into the psyche; the real being inaccessible in language, the imaginary is the phase when the baby attaches itself to an image that reflects a unity on the scattered mental process of the child. The mirror offers the baby a specular "I" that it identifies itself with, but since this image is a fictive totality, the subject will always be in a struggle to fit into this imaginary "I." The symbolic dimension introduces the child into the social order through language in which the phallus as the main signifier forbids the child and the mother from any fulfilment of desire. The phallus signifies the lack in the mother and thus, it orders the subjects in the economy of sexuality (Lacan 1982, 83-84).

Lacan emphasizes the role of language as the indispensable component of the castration complex. For Lacan, sexual difference occurs through entry into language whereby the phallus as the main signifier produces the subjects in language by the criteria of having the phallus or lacking it. Phallus, the male sex comes to mirror the appropriate form in the emergence of sexual difference by producing the male subject whose desire is initiated by lack symbolized by the mother. By entering into the symbolic or language through the reference of the phallus, the male emerges as the subject of desire, having *it* while woman occupies the position of the other, the "not-all," the zero, the object (Lacan 1982, 144). The transition from the imaginary (pre-oedipal) phase into the symbolic order through the forbidding law of the phallus causes a phantasy of unity with the mother in the imaginary stage, which is an imaginary one and the effect of the split that the subject emerges as sexually different. Woman maintains this phantasy of unity, fulfilment functioning as the cause of his desire, the lost object, *object a.* Thus, Lacan solves the enigma of feminity: The woman does not exist (Lacan 1982, 144).[1] Woman occupies the place of the Other, and this place also refers to the place of God and unconscious. Besides securing man's unity, this place also stands for the truth but since there is no other of the other, not only the Other but also truth is phantasy as well (Rose 1982, 48 -50).

The mother, thus, provides a shelter for the signifying system by holding the absence end of signification as phantasy since woman enters the symbolic as absent. Woman comes about as the guarantor of the male presence by her exclusion from the symbolic and is thus impossible for the reason that she is constituted by and in this very exclusion from language.

---

[1] Whereas for Freud, for an understanding of feminity "turn to the poets, or wait until science can give you deeper and more coherent information" (qtd in *Speculum*, 129).

According to Lacan, what makes the speech of woman impossible is that the category of man and woman are subject to language that places the woman to the position of lack. Therefore, by definition in discourse, desire is itself what bars the fulfilment of desire of either woman or man. Unlike Freud who devises a possibility for the satisfaction of desire, which is achieved by taking a wife for man and by reproducing for woman, Lacan claims that the fact that the phallus signifies the lack in the mother relinquishes any logic for sexual desire to be fulfilled; the law forbids the mother and the child from satisfaction. The gendered subject that emerges as the result of this split seeks satisfaction for the very reason that satisfaction does not exist. Sexual pleasure being conditioned on the lack of the female in discourse, it becomes an impossible pleasure, the pleasure doomed to be pursued after because it is impossible. In this order, the only possibility of a relationship between the sexes is courtly love since any relation between the sexes is barred in discourse (Lacan 1982, 141). So man offers his love to an absence (in language) that assures his identity and presence. It is not a woman that he desires but the lack that remained out of discourse; his other that includes all women as his mother who are in return assumed to seek for pleasure in mothering men.

Irigaray's main objection is against the assumption of the masculinity of the libido in the pre-oedipal stage, which assumes that there is only one body, that of the boy's. The belief that the girl does not discover her vagina in the pre-oedipal phases of infantile sexuality takes into account only the penis as the paradigm of sexual desire. Also, since the mother is described as the phallic mother and the girl is a man, the desire is between two phalluses, which projects a male homosexual economy on the mother-daughter relationship (*Speculum,* 31 -32). The theory of castration complex again takes the penis as the standard sexual organ and the appropriate form and relegates the female sexual organ to absence. In this economy, woman is neither acknowledged to have a value in and for herself nor represented as an entity – she is the negative term in subjectivity: man who does not have a penis, not man but aspiring to be a man. The girl's desire for her mother, specificity of her body, her sexuality, her instincts, and her relation to her mother remain unexplained, repressed by the economy governed by the phallus. In this paradigm, the phallus is represented as the guarantor of sexual difference and pleasure, yet, since woman, the other sex, her sexual organs are defined in terms of possessing or lacking the phallus, what happens is not the articulation or theory of sexual difference but the assertion of the value of the phallus. The phallus governs the logic of subjectivity, which Irigaray calls phallomorphism.

This is a one sex configuration in which the theory assumes that there is only one sex attributing to this one sex the only truth and means to realize his desire. Despite the claim of psychoanalysis to explain how woman and man come about, it does not actually take into account the specificity of the female sex by offering the male as the only sex without considering the historical determinants of the social order and theory itself. Psychoanalysis is itself determined by the patriarchal culture which takes the male sexuality as the norm and negates the female sex. What this theory offers as the economy of sexuality is the perfect model needed for the perpetuation of male dominance which requires women to abdicate their mother and thereby their own sexuality to uphold the paternal line. In this theory, for woman to fit into the social structure, she has to renounce and despise her sexual organs, her mother, and her desire for the mother, and replace her desire with the penis-envy whereas the boy's oedipal stage ensures the value of his sexuality through constructing the female as his other that lacks and envies what he has. Woman's invisible sexual organ supports the value of the phallus; the woman who is *really castrated*, without the phallus and conducive to its value by being envious of it.

Woman's repression is evident in the contradictions of this theory: in this scheme, the development of the boy into a normal man is easier and less complicated than that of the girl's. The boy only transfers his desire for the mother to another woman or, in other words, he transfers his desire for the mother into the idea of the mother, and his erogenous zones remain the same throughout his life. On the other hand, the girl is assumed to go through an impossible process in which she changes her object of desire, despises her mother, and desires her father while she has to give up clitoral masturbation and turn to vaginal pleasure. The fact that how the girl accomplishes these changes is not explained shows that woman's instincts and desires are repressed in theory as well as in society.

Desire for the mother is covered up by inscribing the male, the possessor of the phallus as a subject of desire and the only satisfaction left to women is to be the object of male desire. In this phallic appropriation of sexuality, the woman then mime a feminity imposed on her by male desire in order to enter the symbolic (*Speculum*, 59 - 60). She will act as if she had a penis, or in the Lacanian scheme, she will act as if she can satisfy the male and get fulfilment in this way. Having no law, representation, or acknowledgement of her sex and her relationship to her mother, fixes her in the role of the mother and prevents her from relating to other women as different individuals. Represented as the absence in language, language stands in her way as the impasse to an access to subjectivity. As a not man/deficient man, woman lacks an "I" to love herself, other women and men while she constitutes the maternal body on which the male erects his civilization loving his own sex and himself. For the son, since the loss involved in castration is not a real loss but a phantasy of a loss that woman represents in her body, castration complex does not hinder the male from masturbation and the boy perseveres to desire the mother only transferring this desire to a desire for the maternal function (*Speculum*, 81 -82). Therefore, this representation of sexuality that underlies the social order shows that both men and women remain attached to the mother, the maternal body in the symbolic order.

Patriarchal culture based on this economy of desire provides man with the satisfaction of his incestuous desire for the mother by representing all women as mothers while the incest taboo keeps this desire hidden by the pretense of taboo. Similarly, the taboo on virginity makes the incestuous satisfaction possible since the hymen makes men think the virgin as different from the mother while at the same time the violation of the hymen fulfills the male desire to enter the maternal body. The taboo on virginity and incest maintains the exchange of women among men. These taboos veil the rules that govern the society.

Placing theory and psychoanalysis in the historical, social context, Irigaray suggests that the theory of the castration complex soothes the anguish of man (Freud, for instance) in the sight of the vagina, the difference, "a nothing to see," that is not a penis that raises horror and fear in the male who invests his being, truth, and theory on the value of the phallus. The male subject feels ""wounded," threatened by "castration," by anything he cannot see directly, anything he cannot perceive as like himself" and thereby rejects the existence of difference (*Speculum*, 138). If this envy is not imputed on woman and the mother is recognized as woman, man would have to recognize the difference of the other and confront woman as different from himself, which would postulate another economy of desire and therefore another conceptualization of truth as well. Penis-envy functions as a remedy to man's castration anxiety by representing the fear of losing his penis in the female genitals.

Phallocentric psychoanalytic theory reveals that the condition of the continuation of patriarchal order is to secure the name of the father which requires the father-son relationship as the model. The mother-daughter relationship is violated for the sake of the father-son relationship and, thus, men can own women to support the value of the phallus and fulfill their incestuous desire for the mother. Woman has value as long as she sustains the value of the phallus; as the guardian of the phallus, she becomes a commodity to be exchanged among men who need her body, the maternal body for the support of their own identity. In "Women on the Market," Irigaray applies Marx's analysis of commodity on women's status in society and demonstrates that the quality of commodity and women's position are no different. Women are circulated in society among men like commodities that do not speak or claim value on their own, that do not relate to each other except for a relation of contrast in terms of value for men.

As commodities, women have two levels of value: use value that is reproduction, and exchange value that is determined in its relation to an external standard—the phallus. The external standard—gold or currency—permits the comparison of a commodity to another commodity, and the two commodities' relation lies in their relation to the third term. The immanent value of a commodity does not affect their exchange value; it is the phallus as the third term that determines their exchange value. This exchange is indispensable for the maintenance of the economic, social, and cultural order since other exchanges (of money, property, knowledge, etc.) are predicated on exchanging and owning women. The exchange of women forms the model that other exchanges are based on. Accumulating women—the more women the more valuable the phallus is—is the basic model for ownership and accumulation of wealth.

In this economy, women enter society as either mother, virgin or prostitute, none of which allows women their pleasure. The violation of the hymen transmits the virgin who represents the exchange value into use value as mother who is thus excluded from the exchange in order to (re)produce under the name of man (*This Sex*, 185-187). Since in this order men exchange women, commodities, language among themselves, Irigaray states that homosexuality is the basic principle in this society:

> "Heterosexuality is nothing but the assignment of economic roles: there are producer subjects and agents of exchange (male) on the one hand, productive earth and commodities (female) on the other."
>
> The reason for the prejudice against homosexuality is that this order has to keep the rules hidden. Interpreting the rules governing the society openly puts the order in jeopardy so the prejudice against homosexulity among men veils over the hom(m)osexual structure of the order (*This Sex*, 192).

This society based on the father-son relation and on the love and value of the phallus is a man-to-man society where women occupy the position of a commodity. It is in this sense that Irigaray describes patriarchal society as a hommo-sexual society. Woman does not have a subject position to value itself and other women as their only relation is the relation of a commodity to another commodity, which is competition. After Irigaray's critique of psychoanalytic theory of sexuality, now we turn to her reading of deconstruction to see how deconstruction sustains patriarchal culture for Irigaray.

II. De or Re Construction of the Subject

As Irigaray's argument on sexual difference and on the lack of female subjectivity already implies, she has a critical stance towards Derrida's deconstruction of the subject for the reason that it does not bear any concern for the female subject. Deconstruction assumes that deconstruction of the subject eliminates the hierarchy between the male and the female automatically, so the lack of the representation of sexual difference is not actually discussed in Derrida's theory despite the fact that he is indebted to feminism which has initiated the questioning of the universality of the subject by insisting on the social construction of identity. The twentieth century marks the male subject's crisis. However, for women the problem must be put differently since they already lacked this subjectivity and this is because sexual difference is not articulated. In her discussion on the differences and common points between Irigaray and Derrida in *Philosophy in the Feminine*, Whitford argues that deconstruction maintains the same-sex economy of representation making use of the female voice in order to produce multiplicity whereby the woman becomes a *différance* for the male subject to achieve his multiple subject without producing any change in the place of the woman as subject (Whitford 1991, 127-128). Derrida's reported response to a question on the woman's place in the deconstruction of the subject in "Women in the Beehive: A Seminar with Jacques Derrida" illuminates this point:

> The side of the woman is the side from which you start to dismantle the structure. So you can put undecidability and all of the other concepts which go with it on the side of feminity, writing and so on [...] Starting with deconstruction of phallogocentrism, and using the feminine force, so to speak, in this move and then –and this would be the second stage or second level- to give up the opposition between men and women.
> [...]
> Once you have succeeded, the word "woman" does not have the same meaning. Perhaps we could not even speak of "woman" anymore (Derrida 1989, 194-195).

On the other hand, Irigaray does not only speak of woman, she also says that it is necessary that woman and women should speak as well if the purpose is to deconstruct the (male) subject. Reading the underlying imaginary of deconstruction, Irigaray proposes that this deconstructive process uses women as constitutive of the now deconstructed (male) subject by posing the female as the negative of the male; the dark, chaotic, irrational side again (*Speculum*, 133- 137). The male subject colonizes the female subject by turning her into his negative again while denying her entry into the subject position, which means that deconstruction does not change anything for woman or women. The result is that the female supports the male in his deconstruction as she does in his construction of subjectivity and meaning. Deconstruction draws its strength from the model of the same sex. Irigaray explains the deconstruction of the male subject as follows:

The "subject" henceforth will be multiple, plural, sometimes di-formed, but it will still postulate itself as the cause of all the mirages that can be enumerated endlessly and therefore put back together as one. A fantastic, phantasmatic fragmentation. A destruct(tura)tion in which the "subject" is shattered, scuttled, while still claiming surreptitiously that she is the reason for it all (*Speculum*, 135).

The male subject claims the right that only he can speak like a woman to undo himself whereas women remain in silence when the male subject is deconstructing himself. Whitford points out the injustice that is apparent in the different reception of Derrida's claim to speak like a woman and feminists' claim to speak as women. While Derrida can adopt the position of the woman, to write like a woman to prevent from falling back on metaphysics, feminists, especially Irigaray since she has been charged with essentialism, who talk of an identity for woman are assumed to fall back on phallocentricism by speaking like men (Whitford 1991, 132- 134). Whitford explains that "to speak mimetically like a man is not to be a man speaking like a man; it does not elicit the same reactions or produce the same effects" (Whitford 1991, 129). The problem, then, is that, for Derrida, in the domain of writing if women claim a subjectivity, they are phallocentric, and this domain does not have to deal with the social dimension in which women are excluded as subjects again. This means that like all truth, non-truth, the female voice and speaking like a woman is also the privilege of the male subject. Thus, he ends up where he started, the male subject speaking, and the female subject silent, and why he walked all this way to deconstruct the male subject is a question. Woman becomes a place in language that only the male can make use of and thus, Derrida avoids the problem of sexual difference, which leads again to using the female in the maternal function to support his presence/theory.

Deconstruction, then, is not far from the male hom(m)osexual culture in which male subjects exchange and negotiate, and, here, deconstruct the subject; it excludes the female subject who has not posed her question yet. Her question is where her desire, sexuality, sexual organs are placed in this symbolic and how they are constructed in deconstruction. The deconstructionist project's answer to feminism is similar to that of Marx's in the presumption that the proletariat state will automatically abolish women's slavery and their subjection to men, which does not take into account the particularity of women's experience and the male domination. Deconstruction is one of the tools that Irigaray adopts but it is not her project, which becomes clear when she asserts that woman as the subject of her desire and truth must come to existence and deconstruction can only be a step towards this end rather than being an end in itself. Irigaray regards the subjection of the female to the male desire as the foundation of capitalist, destructive society, and of the metaphysics of presence. Therefore, any struggle and deconstruction has to first acknowledge woman as not the Other, hear the silence of female desire, and represent the non-represented woman.

For Irigaray, the aim is to bring about a change in both language and society—she sees change in language indispensable for creating a different social order (*Thinking*). This means that the deconstruction of the subject is possible with the entry of the female subject into language since the male subject is constructed on the absence of woman as a subject. Therefore, the logic of identity, truth, and thought that results from the inclusion of the female subjectivity in language cannot be placed in metaphysics of presence. The entry of the female subject into language is what turns this metaphysics upside down because if woman does not subtend the signification, the production of truth, and the logic of identity is not based on the oneness of the form (of the phallus) or the sameness (of the male), a new language and a new configuration of subjectivity will have to emerge. The charge of essentialism in arguing for a subjective identity for woman stems from the inability to conceive that the female subject as the subject of her desire and truth and liberated from the male desire already subverts the subject definition. In Irigaray's words "[w]hat seems difficult or even impossible to imagine is that there could be some other mode of exchange(s) that might not obey the same logic" (*This Sex*, 158). Hence, for Irigaray, the position of woman needs to change from the position of a commodity in exchange among men.

Though Irigaray's speaking of woman as not one and Derrida's aim of achieving a multiplicity in the subject are similar and share the same stance towards phallocentrism, Irigaray differs from Derrida in that she does not abandon "speaking (as) woman" (*This Sex*, 136). The multiplicity of the female that Irigaray talks about has two aspects; first, in the existent logic of identity that is based on the unity and *oneness* of the form of the phallus, woman is what is left as the excess of the unique male subjectivity. Irigaray states that "The rejection, the exclusion of a female imaginary undoubtedly places woman in a position where she can experience herself only fragmentarily as waste or as excess in the little structured margins of a dominant ideology" (*This Sex,* 30). This is not a celebration of fragmentation. This is the result of the lack of symbolization, representation of female sexual instincts. But also, her access to language and identity would again be multiple; she would not be defined by the logic of phallologism since "woman does not have a sex. She has at least two of them, but they cannot be identified as ones" (*This Sex*, 28). The specificity of the female sex cannot be thought of in the logic of the phallus. Through the allusion to the female sexual organ, the multiplicity of women's erogenous zones, Irigaray states that the identity that woman can have access to should not be perceived from the point of male identity. It should be in accord with the multiplicity of the female pleasure. Criticizing Irigaray for falling back on phallocentrism means assuming that when Irigaray speaks about female subjectivity, she applies the logic of identity to the female subjectivity but Irigaray offers a different conceptualization of subjectivity; one that does not obey the law of phallomorphism. Irigaray does not oppose a female truth or identity against the male subject; she suggests a different conceptualization of truth, representation, and subjectivity.

Now, the question is how can woman speak in a subject position in this symbolic which does not acknowledge woman and her desire? As Whitford puts it, mimicry comes to play an important role in the abeyance that the female finds herself in language (Whitford 1991, 70- 71). Although language is the locus of her repression, women need to use this very language in order to accede to subjective identity. This is what Irigaray does in the magnificent language of *Speculum*. Here, she subverts its logic by displaying, revealing, parodying, unveiling it through abundant repetitions—for instance, "the little girl is a little man," "the dark continent," "magma" and "hysteria," with the expressions that she borrows from Freud. These obliterate the meaning of the repeated expressions, phrases by exposing their logic. Adopting the feminine role deliberately functions as *a technique* for both enabling woman to speak and to overturn the representations, symbols, images that block her way to speech and subjectivity. Irigaray says that:

> One must assume the feminine role deliberately. Which means already to convert a form of subordination into affirmation, and thus to begin to thwart it. [...] To play with mimesis is thus, for a woman, to try to recover the place of her exploitation by discourse, without allowing herself to be simply reduced to it (*This Sex*, 76).

As there is no way out of the symbolic, language, women have to use the (male) language, mimic in order to expose its mechanism that allocates woman to silence or the role of the other. This does not mean submission to the logic of sameness but it is a strategy to effect a change in the symbolic. Whitford suggests that "[t]he tactic of mimesis can be seen as a kind of deliberate hysteria" (Whitford 1991, 71). That is to say, mimicry can be used as a tool to expose the artificiality of the imposed feminine role. Repressing female sexuality in society or in representation does not erase the female desire in language. Irigaray proposes that what is left out of the law/love of the father does not simply vanish but finds ways of resistance and makes itself heard in the silences and gaps in language. In Irigaray's words, language bears "those *blanks* in discourse which recall the places of her exclusion and which, by their *silent plasticity*, ensure the cohesion, the articulation, the coherent expansion of established forms" (*Speculum*, 142, italics in the original). Revealing these blanks and the condition of the coherence of texts opens up a path for a different system of representation in which sexual difference can be articulated. What is needed is "questioning words as the wrappings with which the "subject," modestly, clothes the "female" (*Speculum*, 142). It is necessary to expose the governing imaginary of the syntax and logic of meaning construction in language in order to disrupt the logic of sameness and rationality as defined by the male imaginary.

In *Thinking the Difference*, Irigaray argues that the forgotten, forbidden, silenced mother-daughter relationship needs to enter our culture through religious, cultural, mythical, and social representations so that the desire for/of the mother and women can subvert the language that is essential for a change in the social order. For Irigaray, the question of female subjectivity lies in the logic of discourse that excludes any articulation of female desire, sexual difference, and a subject position for women to participate in any exchange in society. The fact that the production of meaning and representation exploits women by accruing the negativity, the otherness, silence, or lack on woman urges women to reevaluate, challenge, and interpret their position in language in order to express their desire. This accounts for the increasing interest on the part of women in literature both as writers and as critics since the 1970s when gender and representation emerged as the main stake in feminism. Adopting mimicry as a strategy, women have interpreted their subjection to male discourse and literature in order to effect a change in language and representation. Women writers' endeavor to give voice to the silences in language and the exposition of the logic of male discourse has contributed to devising strategies to cope with the impasses of language and literary forms for women.

Having summed up Irigaray's approach to female subjectivity related to language, I will now turn to Atwood, Carter, and Byatt and show how they, as women writers, deal with the problem of women's place in language and literature, and I will discuss how their writing responds to Irigaray's criticism of patriarchal culture and language.

III. Women Writing About Women Writing About Women

Irigaray's criticism of language and the argument for a female subjectivity are more compatible with the themes that are elaborated in the writings of Angela Carter and Margaret Atwood while Byatt presents a different approach to subjectivity in "Morpho Eugenia". As women writers, they all show their concern with female subjectivity by both choosing women characters and by writing on the issue of writing as a woman in the realm of literature that obliges any gender-conscious woman to struggle, discuss, and negotiate with its history. Besides, their use of experimental narrative techniques, allusions to literary criticism, and their use of intertextuality demonstrate the woman writer's uncomfortable and problematic position within literature and language. Atwood and Carter aim at producing a female subjective identity following Irigaray's argument. On the other hand, Byatt differs from Atwood and Carter in that although binary oppositions and the authority of the male subject are the target of criticism in "Morpho Eugenia," the deconstruction is in the Derridean fashion. Woman remains as the other of the male subject and the problem of sexual difference is overshadowed by class and race discrimination.

Angela Carter presents Fevvers as the *New Woman* of the twentieth century who starts her adventures by learning and practicing mimicry and ends up with hysteria that bears the potential for a female subjective identity in *Nights at the Circus*. Without abandoning the law that assigns woman the object position, Fevvers turns her object position into an advantage without disrupting the subject-object dichotomy. Yet, she displays her body in the object position in such an excessive way that this object position becomes a parody of the subject-object dichotomy. What Carter achieves in the characterization of Fevvers is to expose how woman is represented in the discursive logic based on sameness; as the other, a "not all," an anomaly, the excess, the deviant from the logic of identity. The exposition of the construction and vulnerability of subjectivity in language and the subversive power of fiction as observed in Fevvers' creating herself propounds the work on language in order to diverge from phallocentric ideology of identity.

Irigaray's criticism of patriarchy and language reveals itself best in Atwood's presentation of the destructive patriarchal culture and the consequences of the non-representation of mother-daughter relationships. Atwood discloses how language and fiction confine women in the role of maternity and "the world of male drives, a world where she has become invisible and blind to herself, her mother, other women, and even men" (*Thinking*, 112). While language and fiction are exposed as constitutive of subjectivity in male dominated culture, intertextuality and meta-narration investigates a way to engender a female subjectivity. By shifting the subject-object positions in art—the subject of art and art object—and obliterating the borders between the reader and the writer, Atwood overturns the logic of discourse and literature in order to examine the woman writer's problematic position in literature and language. In the conjunction of this disruption of the discursive logic in the frame story and the suspicious paternal heritage against the safe maternal ancestry (of Sabrina) the suggestion of a different conceptualization of female subjectivity arises. Atwood suggests that this new subjectivity recognizes the desire of/for the mother and it will be configured in language in concomitant with the change in the social order which requires the recognition of the maternal line for determining identity.[2]

Byatt poses a stance that is closer to Derrida rather than Irigaray. In "Morpho Eugenia" she deconstructs the subject and the idea of a natural order through the use of metaphor and analogy in Derridean fashion. Yet, the question of female subjectivity and women's exploitation in patriarchal culture is assimilated in the criticism of socio-economic exploitation. Therefore, the rebellion against, or rather, the escape from the socio-economic structure in Bredely Hall that is represented in Adamson and Matilda's setting off for the Amazons at the end of the novella, is not promising in terms of female subjectivity. With this ending, the change in the here and now that Irigaray calls for is postponed to a future in an Eden-like-world. The female, Matilda as a woman writer, acts the role of Eve, the maternal body when she accompanies the son of Adam in his search for the garden of Eden.

It is obvious that without an understanding of the relation to the mother, the desire of/for the mother, and the link between the production of truth in language and the construction of the male and the female, a different subjectivity cannot be achieved. The deconstruction in "Morpho Eugenia" demonstrates that if the unraveling of the authority of the male subject is not accompanied by a configuration of a female subjective identity, woman and man continue to occupy the same places in the symbolic, which makes it impossible to imagine a different concept of truth or language. In this sense, "Morpho Eugenia" occupies a different place in this discussion of female identity, and this is why I will place the chapter on "Morpho Eugenia" published in 1992, at the end although the chronological order requires it to be placed after *Nights at the Circus*, published in 1984, and before *The Blind Assassin*, published in 2001.

---

[2] See Hatice Yurttaş's "Reading The Penelopiad through Irigaray: Rewriting Female Subjectivity" for a similar reading of Irigaray's critique of the representation of female characters in terms of mother-daughter relationships in Atwood's another writing, The Penelopiad and "Desire in *Middlemarch*" (Yurttas 2017a; Yurttaş 2017b).

CHAPTER ONE

NIGHTS AT THE CIRCUS

1.1. *Ludic Mimicry*[3]

Nights at the Circus[4] is a picaresque novel that starts with the "civil" world of London and ends in a primitive village in the tundras of Siberia. With this picaresque structure, Carter presents a quest for female subjective identity concomitant with a way to restructure the male subjectivity that can produce a different epistemology. The narration starts with a review of the ideas and the institutions that these ideas produced in the nineteenth century that jeopardize female identity through the life story of Fevvers, and advances towards the twentieth century to examine the perils the female subject encounters. Meanwhile, Fevvers moves from mimicry to hysteria in her quest.

In the characterization of Fevvers, Carter exposes how woman, sexual difference is represented in the phallocentric logic of identity: a monster, an excess, an object of the gaze, a freak. Fevvers' education on and profession of displaying her body and identity as an art object elaborates on mimicry that Irigaray describes as an imposed feminity on women in phallocentric discourse in which female sexual instincts have no expression, representation or symbols. However, the deliberate and excessive display of Fevvers' identity exposes the artificiality of her construction as woman and expresses the desire of woman for a different subjectivity. This brings her performance closer to hysteria. Irigaray's following remarks on hysteria applies to Fevvers' performance:

> hysteria holds in reserve, in suspension/suffering, something in common
> with the mime that is a sine qua non of sexual pleasure. The problem is
> that the ludic mimicry, the fiction, the "make believe," the "let's

---

[3] This phrase is adopted from Irigaray (*Speculum*, 60).
[4] It will be referred to as *NC* hereafter.

pretend"- which, as we know, made the hysteric subject to all kind of disbelief, oppression, and ridicule-are stopped short, impeded, *controlled by a master-signifier,* the Phallus, and by its representative(s) (*Speculum,* 60, italics in the original).

In this context, Fevvers appears as a hysterical epitomizing the potential for expressing female sexuality and pleasure since hysteria debunks the phallocentric mechanism and its repression of female instincts. Building her identity on the slippery ground of mimicry, Fevvers sets off from the nineteenth century in which she leaves behind a brothel and a museum of woman monsters, hardly escapes sacrifice and marches towards the twentieth century, turning her objectification by the male gaze into her financial and libidinal advantage. Her temporal move accompanies her spatial travel. This nomadic existence in time and space, as Braidotti states, bears a potential for a different configuration of female subjectivity. This quest is not only embodied in Fevvers but it is also indicated through the characterization of Liz who is Fevvers' foster-mother, and their relationship which is not based on the axis of the maternal role.

The Cockney Venus, Helen of the High Wire, Winged Victory, *tableau vivant,* the most famous *aerialiste,* the English Angel, the Virgin Whore, the bird woman are some of the descriptions and stage names tucked on or adopted by the fascinating protagonist of *NC* whose "legal handle"[5] is Sophie but Fevvers is the name that she prefers in her career (Carter 2003, 13). As it is apparent in the names, contradiction is embodied in her. Fevvers' identity is presented as a matter of controversy between fact and fiction. Her identity is always in between the oppositional terms: she is neither fiction nor real, she has got wings like a bird but she is not an animal; she is blonde but she has a masculine grip; she is very big, eats and drinks *too much,* and "guffaw[s]" (7). She is a virgin—or she claims to be a virgin—which marks the exchange value of woman that maintains patriarchal market but she is also a whore that represents the natural, or use value of woman.

Irigaray says that the mother, the virgin, and the prostitute are the social roles that are imposed on women in order to perpetuate the social

---

[5] References to *NC* will be given as page numbers in parenthesis hereafter.

order, but the passage from one to the other is also regulated (*This Sex*, 186). The violation of the hymen or turning from the mother to the prostitute is executed according to the principles of the market, however, Fevvers does not obey this categorization by combining the two contrary identities in her stage name. It is not possible to define her in the oppositional logic; the metaphysics of presence is not applicable to her body. This rejection of being either/or places Fevvers outside the binary logic, Fevvers makes use of mythological figures in distorted versions. First of all, Fevvers mentions that she is hatched like Helen of Troy and like her, she causes chaos and excitement in society, but she is the Helen of the High Wire and her power does not derive from her feminine beauty, but from her own performance. Both Helen and Fevvers' power comes from their body, but while Helen is trapped in the beauty of her body, Fevvers avoids this entrapment by not letting anybody define her body as real or artificial. She is Venus, but a cockney, a working-class goddess. Leda and the Swan appear in the picture in the drawing room of the brothel and Fevvers takes this picture as her "primal scene," her "own conception" (28). The implication that she is the daughter of a woman and a god in disguise of a swan has two suggestions; first she is the medium between a human being and an animal and thereby the medium of the artificial hierarchy devised by the human mind. Second, she is the second chance of woman in the ancient war between men and women. Although Leda and the Swan are usually represented as lovers in the paintings of Michelangelo and Leonardo Da Vinci for instance,[6] the story is that Zeus in the guise of a swan rapes Leda, which is then another incident of the defeat of the woman/the goddess by man/god and the critical moment in the establishment of patriarchy (Whitford 1991, 102-103). After her mother, Leda, is seduced by the male, Zeus, the famous trickster, Fevvers now as the new woman in the twentieth century, tries her chance in the confidence trick to win her power back. This time it is woman who seduces man in disguise rather than being raped or tricked by the male that disguises himself in the form of a swan. In other words, it is now woman's turn to play tricks in the game of disguises and seduction.

---

[6] See the pictures on http://en.wikipedia.org/wiki/Leda_and_the_swan.

Whether Fevvers' wings are real or not stays in the heart of *NC* both for the public, the media, and the men after Fevvers in the novel as well as for the reader—at the beginning at least, for after a while it becomes clear that this controversy is what makes Fevvers. Fevvers' slogan "Is she fact or fiction?" is crucial to her existence. What makes Fevvers the object of desire, attention, commodity is the controversy of this bird woman's bodily features; her very survival and power depends on the conservation of this vulnerable ground in the middle of these two poles. Her performance on stage is carefully devised to keep her identity controversial. Although she is not a trapeze artiste, she does not go higher than an *artiste*; despite her claim to be a real bird woman, she imitates the artificial one.

The play of absence and presence, or fact and fiction that is played upon her body is a dangerous game: the absence of fiction—that is her wings proven to be real—will kill Fevvers as the object of desire. If she is revealed to be an anomaly, she will share the fate of other anomalies in society: the blind, the autistics, people without legs/arms, etc. She will no longer cause excitement. Walser realizes this when Fevvers faces the danger of being fixed in her anomaly as "an alien creature forever estranged" when Charivaris concocts a plot to expose Fevvers (161). On the other hand, if it is proven that her wings are artificial, she will be condemned as a liar, "a humbug" like ordinary liars such as mediums, fortune-tellers, hodjas, etc. In short, Fevvers' life depends on the suspension of disbelief. Defining, stabilizing her identity will kill her. Therefore, she protects herself from being defined as either the one or the other. Walser, the journalist who comes for an interview with her, appreciates her: "She owes it to herself to remain a woman, he [Walser] thought. It is her human duty. As a symbolic woman, she has a meaning, as an anomaly, she has none" (161). To prevent herself from being categorized as an anomaly, a freak, Fevvers maintains her identity dubious.

The feminine items of clothing in Fevvers' dressing-room contribute to the construction of Fevvers' ambiguous identity as a woman. When the items of clothing like silk stockings are displayed dirty in the messy room, they turn the feminity that they represent into a parody of feminity. Fevvers' silk stockings and undergarment no longer look feminine when they are thrown here and there, dirty in the messy room or on Fevvers when she is "unwomanly" guffawing or eating and drinking excessively. Walser's description of her in the dressing room includes a great deal of references to clothing, especially to underwear and stockings, the dirt, and the smell of bodily juices. These descriptions point to the anomaly of this woman or rather her combining both the normal and abnormal in her.

Fevvers uses clothing for hiding her body, her wings when she is not on the stage but this hiding is Fevvers' choice; she will show herself as the object to be looked at when she wants and she will avoid the gaze that wants to know whether her wings are real or not by putting on clothes. For Fevvers, clothing is a tool to manage her reception and perception by others consciously rather than being the wrapping of commodity that is the expensive clothing for raising the value of woman. Nevertheless, this is autonomy rather than independence because she is not in control of the signification of clothing or the identity that goes with different types of clothing. Even though she can hide her wings with shawls, she cannot save herself from being categorized as "hunchbacked", an anomaly with her shawl making a hump on her back (127). The signification of clothing is in the hands of others to define. This shows that her control over her image and identity by her choice of clothing is limited by the boundaries and definitions that are not her own making. The song that goes with her slogan "only a bird in a gilded cage," proves the irony of her situation (14). Her freedom is that of the tropical bird brought to civilization as an expensive object to be kept well and looked after in a cage or in the zoo.

Despite the fact that she has power in society, she is still surrounded, imprisoned by the idea of woman imposed on her. What she can do is to build a space to survive; this is not freedom or rather, this is not to suggest that woman can avoid the object position and accede to female subjectivity by simply blurring the borders of this identity or playing with her own image. Fevvers wants to survive and benefit financially by using her status as a valuable object. Moreover, she even falls back on the role of the victim woman waiting to be rescued by the prince. When desperate in desolate Siberia, she invests her hope in Walser: "I forgot myself so as to cry out: "My young man will come and save us!"

(241). The space that she builds for herself does not necessarily prevent her from falling back on the traditional identity for woman.

In *The Sadeian Woman*, Carter discusses that Juliette in Sade's *Juliette or Vice Amply Rewarded* is a representative of woman who enters the domain of power not in the role of the suffering, chaste, passive victim, but as an active agent (Carter 2001, 78-81). Juliette gains power by proving that she can be as brutal as men, and thereby she achieves a status similar to men. However, the murderous victimizer Juliette can keep this status on the condition that she recognizes men as masters. Carter suggests that she is the model for women of the twentieth century who enter the society and come to power by internalizing the law of society like businesswomen for example: "Juliette transforms herself from pawn to queen in a single move and henceforward goes wherever she pleases on the chess board. Nevertheless, there remains the question of the presence of the king, who remains the lord of the game" (Carter 79). Although she seems triumphant in her avoidance of victimization by patriarchs, Juliette does not threaten the social order since the terms of her entry into power are not her own making. Like Tansu Çiller, Bülent Ersoy or Margaret Thatcher as Munford notes, she can gain financial and libidinal benefit as long as she does not claim or articulate her difference and respects the kings in the games of politics, academy, or the media (Munford 2007, 65). What this powerful woman figure achieves is to avoid victimization and share the male power paying the price of power with denouncing her difference.

The similarity between Juliette and Fevvers, as Munford also highlights, is apparent in Carter's presentation of Fevvers as the new woman of the new century but, as Carter comments on Juliette, "in the mode of irony" (Carter 2001, 79). Carter presents Fevvers as the powerful woman of the twentieth century as an heir to Juliette and her sister Justine who fits the representation of woman as the passive victim in the nineteenth century. In doing this, she demonstrates that the powerful new woman is not much different from the woman represented as victim in that they are both defined by the phallocentric representation system. However, obviously Fevvers is not an aggressive woman like Juliette. In the character of Fevvers, Carter makes an attempt to create an alternative model to Justin and Juliette, which she describes as "a synthesis of their

modes of being, neither submissive nor aggressive, capable of both
thought and feeling" (Carter 2001, 79). For the configuration of such a
synthesis, Carter employs deliberate mimicry and the potentials of hysteria
as the next step of mimicry.

　　Carter plays with the idea of the family by choosing a brothel
where Fevvers grows up as "the common daughter of a half-a-dozen
mothers" (21). Fevvers is a woman without a biological mother and she is
brought up in the brothel by prostitutes who do not fit into the idea of
prostitute created by patriarchal culture. The lack of knowledge as to her
biological origin is not much discussed among the women in the brothel
and she is accepted without jealousy to the house. In the brothel, which
Fevvers describes as an academy, Fevvers gains her first knowledge about
her role as a woman that is prescribed by patriarchal culture. More
importantly, she also learns about solidarity and love among women from
the intellectual, political prostitutes whose representation subverts the
difference between married women and prostitutes.

　　Built in the "age of reason," in the brothel where people thought
"rational desires might be rationally gratified," what is exchanged is not
pleasure but "simulacra" (26; 39); the form of sex that is created as
separate from pleasure. The allusion to Baudrillard's famous term refutes
the idea that sex is repressed; rather, a form, a representation is created
that replaces the sexual pleasure. The women in the brothel sell a copy of
pleasure since pleasure "has no existence unless given freely," yet they
must keep the pretense of giving sexual pleasure since patriarchal culture
is founded on pretenses like the incest taboo and interdiction of
homosexuality (39; *This Sex*, 192-193). Schooling being never mentioned,
Carter chooses a brothel which is like a women's commune for the
education of the new woman instead of a family structure in which a girl
can only learn to obey the law of the father and become a mother like her
mother.

　　The fact that Fevvers' wings grow in puberty concomitant with
her menstrual periods makes her wings a sign of her womanhood. Her
wings and her ability to fly also give her anxiety. When she is on the roof
about to perform her first flight, she realizes that her wings, or her sex is
her *"difference"*: "I feared a wound not of the body but the soul sir, an
irreconcilable division between myself and the rest of humankind" (34,

italics in the original). Fevvers' wings symbolize woman's attempt at liberation from the idea of woman that is tied to her reproductive function and identified with nature. This idea is articulated by Liz upon coming across a mother and her baby isolated in a hut in Siberia: ' this tableau of a woman in bondage to her reproductive nature system, a woman tied hand and foot to that Nature which your physiology denies, Sophie, has been set here on purpose to make you think twice about turning from freak into a woman" (283). Fevvers is hopeful about the twentieth century in which women's body; *nature* will resist the phallocentric definition. She believes that the mother who is left sick with her baby in a shelter in the primitive tribe, for instance, will "have wings" and "fly away" (285). The release from the reproductive function refers to the availability of contraceptives and the law permitting abortion, which facilitated women's entry into the public domain in the twentieth century (which can be put the other way around as well, that the changing needs of the capital needed women's labor in certain areas and so it required use of contraceptives and abortion). Liberation from obligatory motherhood makes it possible for women to gain an identity other than the mother. However, Fevvers' adventures prove that this is not that easy. Even though she gains advantage and protects herself from being captured in the idea of woman, she is still a sign in the "symbolic exchange in the market-place" as Liz puts it, alluding to Irigaray's argument of the exchange of women (185).

After Fevvers "serve[s] [her] apprenticeship in *being looked at*" in Ma Nelson's brothel, by "mimicking" Cupid for the customers, she becomes a professional in the art of performing an identity as the object of the male gaze (23, italics in the original). Moreover, she turns her object position as a woman in the male-dominated society into advantage by overemphasizing the subject-object dichotomy. She presents the audience with a spectacle woman to wonder at:

> Look at me! With a grand, proud, ironic grace, she exhibited herself before the eyes of the audience as if she were a marvelous present too good to be played with. Look, not touch.
>   She was twice as large as life and as succinctly finite as any object that is intended to be seen, not handled. Look! Hands off! (15).

By representing Fevvers as an object of the gaze, Carter actually demonstrates what woman turns out to be in phallocentric discourse. Her interpretation of 'arse-licking' in Sade's work applies to Fevvers' identity as an art object: this is "metaphor made concrete" (Carter 86). Woman's position of excess, objectification, exclusion from the logic of identity based on phallomorphism is embodied in Fevvers. In this economy of representation, woman becomes an art object. Braidotti suggests that woman and monsters share a similar status in society and in the discursive logic for the reason that they both occupy the same place in the symbolic as signs of difference. Braidotti explains that monsters

> represent the in between, the mixed, the ambivalent [...] both horrible and wonderful, object of aberration and adoration. Since the nineteenth century, following the classification system of monstrosity by Geoffroy Saint-Hilaire, bodily malformations have been defined in terms of excess, lack, or displacement of organs (Braidotti 1994, 77 -78).

Both the monster and the woman are pushed towards the margins away from the norm. Braidotti states that the male body is taken as the human norm starting with Aristotle who places the female body as a variation from the normal production of the male body, and now in the psychoanalytic theory of Lacan and Freud that defines woman as the residue of the symbolic allocating her the role of the other (of man) or the status of lack in language, male sexuality is considered as the norm. The category of woman receives the same aggression, repulsion and, at the same time, attraction as the monster that differs from the normal human body. Both the monster and the woman are marginalized as deviant by the phallocentric concept of identity.

In this sense, Madam Schreck's museum of woman monsters exposes the similar fate of physically different people and woman. In the museum, women are exhibited as pure idea of difference. Like the brothel, the museum of woman monsters represents the alternative institutions for woman in the nineteenth century. The museum of woman monsters differs from the brothel in that what is sold in the museum is not sex and the body of woman but the idea of sex and woman. It is not only that desire is separated from sexuality, but also, as Michael states, sexuality is replaced by its representation (Michael 1994, 510). And, customers' not making sex with the women in the museum shows that woman is replaced by the idea of woman which is not different from the idea of monsters. Fevvers leaves behind and also grows out of these two places that belong to the nineteenth century learning that as a woman she has to protect herself from the idea of woman in the male-dominated society since both her body and identity can become a commodity in the market. Her next station is the circus. The circus is different from this museum only in that it is the institutionalized, legal, modern version of exhibiting what is different; the display of animals and the abnormally formed bodies in Europe that Braidotti mentions in her discussion of freaks whose precursors are the monsters (Braidotti 1994, 91).

Setting off from her hometown, London, Fevvers travels to St Petersburg and to Siberia; moving from the familiar, realistic depictions of London to the strange, fantastic, primitive world of Siberia. This movement in space attending her travel through the institutions and dangers for woman symbolizes her search for a different female subjectivity. According to Boehm the picaresque structure itself has "the intention of transforming the representation of women" (Boehm 1995, 4). In *Nomadic Subjects*, Braidotti argues that the figure of nomad as an epistemological position can enable a female subjectivity and discourse that can embody sexual difference. She states that the image of the nomad is "a figuration for the kind of subject who has relinquished all idea, desire, or nostalgia for fixity. This figuration expresses the desire for an identity made of transitions, successive shifts, and coordinated changes, without and against an essential unity" (Braidotti 1994, 22). Fevvers' affinity for a nomadic identity finds expression in her "special fondness" for Bizet's Carmen and her resistance against the definition of her body associates her with nomadic consciousness that Braidotti suggests for feminist politics (54).

Her travel and adventures with Liz, like a female Quixote and Sancha Panza as Fevvers puts it, shows a progress towards chaos and disintegration in the vastness of Siberia (245). In this move towards catastrophe, Fevvers undergoes a spiritual change as well. In St Petersburg, in the Grand Duke's palace, she learns that the price for being seduced by diamonds is to become a jewellery herself in a glass cage, and upon this lesson, she abandons her greed for money and throws the diamonds that the Grand Duke gave her out of the window of the train for little Ivan to take to his grandmother (193). Furthermore, having seen her sword, which she inherited from Ma Nelson, being broken easily by the Grand Duke, she learns that she cannot gain anything by claiming equality or by aspiring to phallic power. She accepts that she does not have the phallus or possessing a similar tool will not help her. Instead of, as Liz says, "pretend[ing] to be an ordinary gal" and flirting "with the adversary," she learns to own her difference, that is, her womanhood (198).

Although this traveling and change in the experience of traveling makes her resemble a picaresque character that matures after the adventures *he* goes through, she is a female picaro different from the male one-like Tom Jones for instance- in that after her travels she is not incorporated into the social structure like the male picaro (Fielding 1992). Instead, she advances to the margins of society both physically and symbolically in a primitive village in Siberia with a witchlike woman companion and a man who is at the beginning of devising an identity and past for himself, learning *to be*. Unlike the male picaresque hero, Fevvers' traveling does not end in being incorporated into society by marriage; her traveling takes her farther from the social order without reaching a stable condition.

Accompanying Fevvers' "moral growth" out of her greed for money as Liz puts it, in Siberia, Fevvers also faces her bodily vulnerability; her wings may break, her colors may fade, and when her wings lose their strength and brightness, she loses her confidence in herself (282). She becomes an ordinary being, "a crippled wonder," a *normal anomaly* (273). She attributes the cause of her misfortunes and loss of magnificence to losing her sword (273). When it is considered that the sword symbolizes phallic power, what happens in Siberia without an audience to perform for is that Fevvers, woman relinquishes mimicry or more correctly, she has to relinquish it because she sees that mimicry is a dangerous, vulnerable strategy. Yet, how to be without mimicry is a question that Liz and Fevvers debates at the end without reaching a conclusion (279-282). This debate opens the last section titled "Siberia," and it unveils Fevvers' confusion about what to do if not resemble what she is miming. The question is mostly related to Fevvers and Walser's end, the relationship between man and woman. What will become of the new woman or man is at stake as the journey nears the twentieth century. Fevvers is optimistic about man:

> [...] I will transform him. You said yourself he [Walser] was unhatched, Lizzie; very well- I'll sit on him, I'll hatch him out, I'll make a new man of him. I'll make him into the New Man, in fact, fitting mate for the New Woman, and onward we'll march hand in hand into the New Century-" (281)

And Liz is cautious "Perhaps safer not to plan ahead" (281). Although the union of lovers, Fevvers and Walser, in the end looks like "the customary ending of the old comedies of separated lovers, misfortune overcome, adventures among outlaws and savage tribes" as Liz ironically states, Fevvers' spiritual growth and the transformations that Walser undergoes leaves the reader with hope in the future of the new woman. Fevvers' mimicry in "London" and "St Petersburg" turns into hysterical babbling about what to do next in "Siberia."

Walser is also a picaro who starts his literal as well as spiritual journey which is initiated by desire for Fevvers. The first thing Walser learns when he joins the clan of clowns is "the freedom that lies behind the mask, with dissimulation, the freedom to juggle with being" and the experience of "humiliation" which the Colonel states as the first thing about clowning (103; 102). The journalist, who once went to Fevvers to drop her mask, learns about the nature, dangers, and irony of wearing masks. Like Fevvers, now he is in the profession of show and performing identity for the audience which is learning the art of "juggling with being," creating an identity with make-up, costumes, and performance in order to satisfy the audience's desire. This is the profession of the play of being, yet this is no fun for the one who wears the mask since one becomes a clown "when all else fails" as Buffo the Great preaches (119). Walser learns that the appearance that is offered to the audience can also be the tragedy of the being behind the mask. What entertains the audience in the clowns' last performance when Buffo goes mad and Walser barely avoids being killed by him is actually pain and panic. While the clowns make up an identity for the audience, this make-up traps them in return. In this sense, the clowns' tragedy functions as a warning to mimicry. The identity behind the mask can assimilate what is behind it. They become the prisoners in the mask that they themselves created. In this experience, Walser learns to take performances seriously. In the circus, Walser also learns not to take his identity as a human being as the norm and he confronts the difference (of animals). Walser's sense, if not awareness, of the irony in the scenes in which the monkeys turn him into a sample of human anatomy in their serious lesson, and while the Strongman produces *bestial* voices during his sexual intercourse with Mignon, manifests itself in his allusion to *Hamlet*: "What a piece of work is man! How noble in reason! How infinite in faculty!" (111). Similarly, dancing with a tigress that leads him in the waltz since he does not know how to dance once more curtails his pride in his humanity. Through these experiences, Walser's sense of identity and the norms with which he tested others or the other are disrupted.

The next station for Walser is his apprenticeship with the shaman in the primitive tribe in Transbaikalia. The amnesia and the re-entry into the symbolic complete his change. Now, Walser has learned that reason is an artificial construct and what is taken to be real and true depends on the ideology or the mythology of a subject or society. Thereby, in the end, he gives up applying reason in order to define Fevvers who is now naked washing herself when he sees that Fevvers "*appeared* to possess no navel" (interestingly her body is still not clear) (292; italics mine). Walser now starts all over in a new way to start an interview; now the male wants to learn her name; to hear her story rather than imposing on her his own rationality or idea of woman. The change in female subjectivity is thus accompanied by the change in the male subjectivity; man now can confront and accept Fevvers' difference or sexual difference. He overcomes the fear of castration that results in his denial of and aggression towards woman, and thereby he learns the meaning of fear as it defines itself in its most violent form, that is, fear of the death of the beloved, of the loss of the beloved, of the loss of love. It was the beginning of an anxiety that would never end, except with the deaths of either or both; and anxiety is the beginning of conscience, which is the parent of the soul but is not compatible with innocence (292).

What is needed is epistemology that recognizes desire, love; a painful and an erotic one at the same time, to get himself "scrape upon scrape," to break "the shell of unknowing" of difference. The male/the son, then needs to gain his subjectivity not through the fear of the loss of the phallus, but through the fear of the loss of love/the mother so that he does not have to refuse the mother an existence and a subjectivity. Knowledge (of desire), the loss of innocence (which can equate the rejection of the mother) for the growth of conscience makes the laugh of woman possible. Walser's new way of looking at Fevvers' body, his learning to love and look differently marks the dawn of a different epistemological subject that can create a different discourse. Desire, love is not excluded from this new mode of knowing, on the contrary, it is what creates a new epistemology. Irigaray says that the meaning of philosophy does not have to be the love of wisdom; it can also be translated as the wisdom of love since grammar allows this (She illustrates this with the terms zoophilia and theology; the love of animals, and discourse on God respectively). Philosophy does not have to detach itself from love, the wisdom that can be gained through, by, with, in love (*The Way*, 1-4). At the end of *NC* is a potential for a different *being* and a new root of epistemology; Carter proposes that instead of appropriating the other into one's subjectivity, oneness through negating, dehumanizing the other, love, acceptance of difference, and letting the other *be* is the foundation of a different subjectivity and epistemology.

It is true that Fevvers mimics a work of art and offers herself as a *tableau vivant*, but this is her mask like a shell that she has to wear to protect herself: "I was as if closed up in a shell, for the white would harden on my face and torso like a death mask that covered me all over, yet inside this appearance of marble, nothing could have been more vibrant with potentiality than I!" (39). She does not feel that comfortable with mimicry, and moreover, there is potential for creating another identity behind the mask. However, masks can replace the original.Fevvers is in danger of being frozen in her appearance; the mask can eternalize itself and relinquish the self behind it. Mimicry is the edge of the knife: on the one side is the potentiality, on the other, death (of difference, pleasure). Liz warns Fevvers that she "grow[s] more and more like [her] publicity'" when Fevvers invests too much on Walser. Considering her awareness of her position in society—that she is defined by the objectifying male gaze and discourse—the characterization of Fevvers can be interpreted as a phase in creating a subjective identity for woman. She is herself aware of the potentiality of herself but she does not know yet what to make of her identity as a woman. When Liz accuses her of resembling what she mimes, Fevvers expresses her helplessness: "well, who *am* I supposed to be like, then, if not meself" (198). Liz tells her that she has to find this out for herself: "You never existed before. There's nobody to say what you should do or how to do it. You are Year One. You haven't any history and there are no expectations of you except the ones you yourself create" (198). Woman has no history, no models, and no definition to rest against. While she mimes the feminity that is imposed on her, she has to find a way to realize the *vibrant potentiality of the "I"*. Leaving the brothel and the museum of woman monsters and the circus behind, the female picaro continues her adventures to search for subjectivity that can let her live her pleasure.

Irigaray says that in the economy of representation that does not allow symbols and signs for the female desire except for mimicry, symbols of the female instincts and desire appear in dreams and in hysteria which is the psychological disturbance that shows physical symptoms as well. Irigaray's discussion of neurosis (or hysteria) as explained by phallocentric psychoanalysis helps to understand Fevvers' offering herself as a work of art and her reception:

> Woman's special form of neurosis would be to "mimic" a work of art, to be *a bad (copy of a) work of art.* Her neurosis would be recognized as a counterfeit or parody of an artistic process. It is transformed into an aesthetic object, but one without value, which has to be condemned because it is a *forgery.* It is neither "nature" nor an appropriate technique for re-producing nature. Artifice, lie, deception, snare- these are the kinds of judgments society confers upon the tableaux, the scenes, the dramas, the pantomimes produced by the hysteric (*Speculum*, 125, italics in the original).

Fevvers' consciously displaying herself as a work of art is the form that female desire takes in phallocentric economy of representation. The excess that marks everything about her—her size, eating and drinking habits, the abundant hair, the big eye lashes—makes her, as Kérchy calls, "the revolutionary hysteric who rejects the homogenous cultural identity [...] who tries to translate herself into another idiom [...] testing the limits of body, identity and symbolic representation alike" (Kérchy 2004, 115).

Walser's aim in his interview to prove that she is a humbug is the expression of his aggression towards and denial of female desire. He appeals to reason, scientific knowledge in order to define Fevvers' body, which means to place her within the social order and reject her different desire. His disbelief in her shows his denial of the existence of woman other than the one *he* defines.

The dangers that Fevvers faces in her travels and the various reactions towards her from mockery to turning her into the object of science reinforce the parallel between Fevvers and the hysteric as explained by Irigaray. It is not only wonder and attraction that Fevvers arouses in society. She is also the target of aggression. The reason for this aggression towards the hysteric is that the hysteric or Fevvers' appearance exceeds the logic of identity and defies what is accepted as natural. In addition to her challenge to the concept of nature, she disrupts the rules of the exchange of women. Fevvers does not let her virginity to be used as an exchange value. She is famous with her virginity and this means that she does not enter the exchange market in order to become the use/natural value as a mother (*This Sex*, 185-186). Her claim for recognition in her *unnatural, illegal* identity reveals the *forgery* in her representation as woman.

Irigaray says that the reason behind the aggressiveness to the forgery displayed by the hysterical is also that the hysteric reminds of red blood which connects individuals to the mother. However, the significance of red blood jeopardizes the culture for it is established on the prohibition of blood as a symbol of the link to the mother and maternal line. Sperm replaces the red blood for the definition of identity and heritage when patriarchy is established in order to secure the name and property of the father. The repression of blood of woman, virgin, mother, however cannot be accomplished and the taboo on blood finds expression in sado-masochistic practices. By shedding the blood of the mother, virgin man will taste the pleasure of transgressing the taboo and he will also command blood by being the active agent over it. Blood will lose its authority in the male imaginary (*Speculum*, 125 - 126). This explains Rosencrautz's attempt to sacrifice Fevvers. By shedding her blood, he will dominate woman, absorb her in his identity.

If Fevvers is trapped in the imagination of the viewer and defined by it, she suspects herself. She asks "Am I fact? Or am I fiction? Am I what I know I am? Or am I what he thinks I am?" as she faces the danger of moving "from a woman into an idea" when her body, her presence is defined by the shaman in Siberia as a spirit in his belief system and by Walser as the imagined woman that secures his sense of identity (289). The shaman attempts to trap her when he takes her as an idea, a spirit in his own religious mythology, which means that what Fevverswill be the shaman's idea of her. In other words, as a woman, she will be authored by the male gaze to function in the viewer's system of meaning as the negative, the other, the zero. It gives her shivers "[…] when mages, wizards, impresarios came to take away her singularity as though it were their own invention, as though they believed she depended on their imagination in order to be herself. She felt herself turning, willy-nilly, from a woman into an idea" (289). Fevvers escapes this definition of woman in phallocentric representation by showing her wings and receiving the breath of wonder and thereby asserting her difference. In this way, she proves to the shaman that she is not what he imagines her to be. She must prevent herself from being placed in a belief or thought system by destroying each idea of her, of woman, that the others locate her in by asserting her difference against the idea. That she achieves this by causing wonder recalls Irigaray's interpretation of the concept of wonder as the basic human passion described by Descartes. Irigaray suggests that the feeling of wonder is what frees the other, sexually different from being enclosed in the subject's or the viewer's idea of the other: "This other, male or female, should surprise us again and again, appear to us *new, very different* from what we knew or what we thought he or she should be. […] *Who art thou? I am* and *I become* thanks to this question" (*An Ethics* 64, italics mine).

Then, Fevvers' wish to create wonder in the viewer is her desire to be the other, not the other of the male subject or his unconscious but the other as sexually different woman. Interestingly, the question that Irigaray mentions for the advent of the liberation of the other from one's own definition is similar to the question that Walser asks Fevvers "What is your name? Have you a soul? Can you love?" at the end of his adventures. These questions mark the beginning of Walser's change, which Fevvers welcomes joyfully. Now, instead of approaching Fevvers, the other, woman in order to impose on her his idea of her, as he does at first in the dressing room, he wants to hear what she will say about herself.

The relationship between Fevvers and Liz which is not based on the maternal function gives hope in the potentiality of the "I" that mimics a desire that is not her own. The nature of their relationship remains obscure but what is certain is that this relationship is not the one in which women become antagonistic towards each other acting out the maternal role. Their relationship is free from the rivalry between women. Although her bringing up Fevvers like a substitute daughter makes Liz a kind of mother to Fevvers, she is also a lover, teacher, and a sister to her. The ambiguity of their relationship is also recognized by Walser who when interviewing Fevvers in her dressing room, takes Liz as Fevvers' dresser, and when he watches the two women walking hand in hand in the street, he realizes that Fevvers looks like Liz's mother due to her big size. Yet, the tale-telling in the dressing room like Scheherazade and her sister make them seem like sisters while they also seem to be lovers because they walk hand in hand and sleep in the same bed. Also, Liz becomes a "bird-mother" to her when she helps Fevvers learn to fly and also in their travels when Liz warns and guides her (32). The fact that they do not relate to each other through a man, a father or husband, makes it possible for them to recognize each other as individuals. Both of them fatherless (or at least the fathers do not appear) and single, their identities are not defined by the phallus as the signifier of their place in society and their relation to each other. In other words, they can relate to each other or exchange (love, respect) because they are not reduced to commodities by the third external term, man (*This Sex*, 175). Their argument about the Duke is a case in point. The Duke's insistence that Fevvers come alone when he invites her, which means without Liz as she is Fevvers' well-known companion, shows that men separate women. Fevvers and Liz have a severe argument over the Duke's intervention. Fevvers is in her rudest mood towards Liz when Liz does not want her to go alone: "Once and for all, you're not to come with me, hobbling along like a rotten old procuress the way you do, you old cow" (181). Then, Walser's entrance into their lives and Fevvers' interest in him also creates distress between them.

Here, love is made possible in the relationship between Fevvers and Liz by putting the mother-daughter relationship on a new and 'unnatural' level. Liz's role in Fevvers' life is more than mothering—that is nourishing, cleaning, and bandaging the wounds;she is also a teacher, sister, lover, even an enemy sometimes. Unlike the women in The *Blind Assassin*[7], *as will be discussed in the next chapter,* who transform all roles into mothering, Liz combines all these roles in her acting: Miss Violence the teacher, Reenie the caring mother, Liliana the biological mother, and Adelia the emblem of tastes and culture. Liz is none of them; since whatever role they play, the women in *BA* remain as mothers in all their roles. What enables Fevvers and Liz to love and respect each other is that they are not attached to a family. Fevvers does not go through the development a girl does, which results in ending up with the inability of self-love or love of the other as a result of replacing the mother in order to gain a status—and thereby she is free from the confusion of herself for Liz—of love and hatred. The differentiation from the mother figure generates self-love that is love among women.

Like Fevvers, Liz also carries an ambiguity as to her identity. First of all, her age is obscure, Walser calculates as "any age between thirty and fifty" (13). She finds Fevvers after her miscarriage, but nothing is mentioned about the father of her baby. As to her origins, we know that she is Italian and according to Fevvers she is from a "family of anarchist bomb-makers" (225). The rest is contradictory bits and pieces about her life story in the narrative that does not give any clear information. Besides the uncertainty of her past, her political line is vague as well. While she is knowledgeable and involved in a political activity, her political stance is difficult to define. She seems closer to Marxist feminism in her conviction that the material conditions produce the power relations and individuals in the world, as it is understood in her discussion with the anarchist in Siberia, but her tendency to anarchism is also obvious and it is made clear when Fevvers mentions that she attended Godwin and Wollstonecraft Debating Society (241). In addition, she never shows any interest in any men and she is very critical of them. Yet, it is not possible to place her in the position of a radical feminist either. When she hears of the woman

---

[7] *The Blind Assassin* will be referred to as *BA* hereafter.

commune in Siberia, she points out to the impracticality of such a society due to the question of male babies (240). Like her age and her past, her political opinions are difficult to define either. What is certain about her is that she is very wise and talented, and she helps Fevvers survive as a woman.

The pamphlets that change hands between Liz and a 'gypsy' woman (150) and the dispatches that Liz sends to London are explained at the end by Liz. We learn that Fevvers is making money to finance "the struggle," which comes as a shock to the reader (282). Moreover, the tour to Russia with the circus is a disguise, which is implied by Liz's anxiety about her mail to London, about "whether the comrades in London got hot news of the struggle" (234). Also, they show solidarity with women against what Fevvers calls "[t]he cruel sex" (155). Despite her jealousy of Mignon, Fevvers provides her with clothes and a position in the circus as the partner of the princess. They are political activists but like Fevvers' body and Liz's identity, their line is not easy to define in the existent classification.

In the representation of Liz as a witch, Carter offers a criticism of rationality that is entangled with the construction of gender and the oppression of female instincts. The conceptualization of rationality stems from woman's fantastically constructed (imagined) body, and woman's exclusion from the logic of identity that takes the male sex and pleasure as norm that governs the symbolic. On her discussion of Irigaray's criticism of rationality, Whitford states that "Within this sexual symbolism, the determinate, that which has form or identity, belongs to the other half of the pair, and is therefore male. Within this schema, rationality falls on the determinate and male side" (Whitford 1991, 66 -67). The construction of woman and rationality occurs at the same move. Female supports rationality of the male subject by holding the opposite, irrational side. When woman is constructed as not-man, she also becomes the irrational as opposed to the rational man. In *NC*, Carter represents witchcraft as a female science, knowledge that has been forgotten and moreover excluded from the domain of knowledge and rationality. Carter seems to be inspired by the witch Durand in Sade for the characterization of Liz. Her commentary on Durand and the root of Liz's abilities as reported by Fevvers are very similar. Fevvers says that "it's too much rationality as procured her [Liz] not altogether undeserved reputation, for when she puts two and two together sometimes she comes up with five, because she thinks quicker than most" (225). And Carter states that Durand "used the formal methods of reason to become a witch. Durand's primal powers are precisely those of enlightenment and reason, put at the service of nihilism. [...] Durand has mastered this world so well that she can foretell the future [...]" (Carter 2001, 93). Liz's implausible abilities like imprisoning Walser in the dressing room and procuring illnesses on Charivaris become plausible when some details in these scenes are considered. That in the dressing room Liz makes tea for Walser shows that Liz has the knowledge of plants and herbs, which is the root of cookery. What is taken to be impossible is actually the root of what is taken as science, the product of rational thinking that is medicine, since modern medicine is based on the knowledge of plants and herbs as well.[5] Although witchcraft is thought to be the opposite of science, logic, Carter shows that it is an alternative medicine -to borrow the popular term of today- of ancient times. Fevvers confides in the reader that

> Shrinkings and swellings and clocks running ahead or behind you like frisky dogs; but there's a logic to it, some logic of scale and dimension that won't be meddled with, which alone she [Liz] keeps the key of [...]
>
>   Her 'household' magic, she calls it. What would you think, when you saw the bread rise, if you didn't know what yeast was? Think old Liz was a witch, wouldn't you! And, then again consider matches! Lucifers; the little wooden soldiers of the angel of light, with whom you'd think she was in complicity if you'd never heard of phosphorus (199).

Following her maternal ancestors, Medea and Circe, Liz practices the female science that is left as residue in patriarchal science's domination. The contents of Liz's handbag as the emblem of her power are never mentioned but from her grudging looks at the shaman's sister's bag that consists of plants she uses as medicine, it is clear that she uses plants for magic (293). What makes witchcraft accepted as unreal is the fact that it is now left out of the logic/the male symbolic as irrational, residue. The witch-hunt in the 15th century is the severest attack on female knowledge and woman that this symbolic has produced. Yet, women, although they have forgotten their roots still keep and use their knowledge especially in small towns and villages in which grandmothers have a deep knowledge of rare plants to cook and weird ways with plants to cure illnesses. However, the methods to cure illnesses are degraded by the patriarchal science whose forefathers are the witch hunters. Witchcraft is also the forbidden knowledge of the female body like the menstrual blood, the pieces that come with the birth of a child that are proven to have curing affects. It is significant that these are what are excluded from the symbolic, *object a*, for they exceed the logic of identity that belong to woman (*This Sex*, 90; 108 -111). This criticism of rationality can also be found in Irigaray's comments on the time when the mother-daughter couple was respected and formed a model for society:

> The mother-daughter couple safe-guarded human food and the site of oracular speech. This couple preserved the memory of the past, and thus the daughter respected her mother, her ancestry. This couple was also concerned with the present: the earth produced food in peace and quiet. It was possible to foresee the future thanks to women's relationship with the divine, with oracular speech (*Thinking*, 13)

Although Liz's maternal ancestry is never mentioned, and she is not a mother, her comradeship with Fevvers appears to have given her the insight into the wonders of nature. The transformation of women's wisdom of nature into witchcraft reflects the way colonization works. In colonization, the previous system, traditions are not erased completely or repressed but they are transformed into a form that is consistent with the new system. When patriarchal science takes over, women's practice becomes an emblem of their illiteracy. Women's power of their mastery of plants threatens the male-dominated society and it results in depreciating this wisdom while using the same knowledge as the base for its science. The knowledge that that has been refused legitimacy, though, emerges as alternative medicine such as homeopathy, naturopathy, chiropractic, and herbal medicine. The knowledge that we do not possess anymore gives Liz power to procure illness on people and also cure illnesses.

Carter represents the shaman and the male religion that he epitomizes as Liz's or female science's counterpart. Like Liz, he can cure illnesses but the secrets of his profession that he confides in Walser show that his belief system is based on the invisible, spiritual world. Thanks to his special inheritance, he claims to see spirits that ordinary people cannot see. Because of people's inability to see these spirits, he is a master of illusions. He has to produce a mouse, for instance, when needed- since without seeing, his people would not believe that a mouse is causing the illness (263). While Liz uses her knowledge of nature, the shaman obtains his power and authority from the invisible, spiritual world. Liz and the shaman represent the female and the male; the domain of the sensible and the domain of the intellectual. Irigaray states that the division between the sensible, the body, nature and transcendental, invisible, celestial is founded on the *division of labor* between the female and the male whereby the male constructs the spiritual domain by taking the maternal body as his ground of subjectivity. Woman's configuration as the guardian of the flesh, representing the corporal and man's equation with spirituality and the mind produces the male subject as a rational being (Whitford 1991, 140-143). When this economy of sexuality and representation deprives women of a subjective identity, women and their contribution to society and science are also depreciated. In this society, Irigaray says that

> The cultural functions that women might have performed have been judged asocial and hence have been barred to them. They were accused of being *witches* and *mystics*, because of the potency of the relations they maintained with the cosmos and the divine, even though they lacked any extrinsic or intrinsic way to express them, or express themselves (*An Ethics*, 97).

Carter, then, gives voice to woman and her science with the representation of Liz instead of alienating and pushing her away from rationality. Moreover, by bringing the shaman, the representative of the master of the invisible world and Liz, the mistress of the visible world together in the implementation of a new ritual of mother-baby care at the end of the novel, Carter implies the potential of a symbolic place or a place in the symbolic order for what Irigaray calls the sensible transcendental (Whitford 1991, 142-144). This term roughly refers to a subjectivity that allows the female a language, symbols, signs, rituals and spirituality to achieve her subjectivity and accede to her pleasure with a different conceptualization of the corporal and the spiritual. However, *NC* leaves this part with an ironic tone—with Liz's repression of "the temptation to take- just this once, just for the night—a little holiday from rationality and play at being a minor deity" on the shaman's addressing Liz "as 'the little mother of all the bears,'" and does not pursue the implications of the synthesis of the spiritual and corporal (293).

1.2. Story Telling: The Ancient Witchcraft

The dense intertextuality of *NC* in terms of allusions to other literary texts and genres like picaresque, *bildungsroman*, and oral tradition in addition to the proliferating stories narrated by Fevvers and by the third person narrator renders *NC* a meta-narration. This meta-narration reveals the creative power of fiction and language besides providing a criticism of literature and genre boundaries. *NC* suggests that subjectivity is an artificial construct in language in which the male forms his subjectivity and truth on a fantasy of the female as his other, and the female lacks a language, subjective identity to express her desire. Through the complicated narrative in which Fevvers appears as both a writer and an art object, and Walser appears as a reader first and then a writer with the position of the reader (us) shifting with each arrangement, Carter destabilizes the subject-object dichotomy in art. This fluctuation in the narrative together with references to other works of literature evinces the woman writer's exile in literary tradition that deprives her of an active subject position. After a well-detailed criticism of language and patriarchy, Carter ends the novel with a potential female subject who has given up mimicry and is hysterical now. Fevvers' disturbance because she does not know what to do when she does not mime the feminity imposed on her shows hysterical symptoms at the end. Fevvers' disturbance and tension in the last section is also reflected on her body; one of her wings is broken and her feathers fade. She relinquishes mimicry, which means that she wants to live and express her desire, but she does not know how. This disturbance implies the criticism of genre as well since genre does not offer any alternative ending apart from the marriage institution.

The first chapter of *NC* named "London" introduces the theme of story-telling through Fevvers' telling her *autobiography* in collaboration with Liz. They appear like Scheherazade and her sister in *The Thousand*

and One Nights in which Scheherazade with her sister tells stories to the prince in order to prevent the prince from killing her. In *The Thousand and One Nights*, Scheherazade saves her life and prevents the prince from killing other women on their bridal nights by manipulating the prince through the power of her stories. This allusion gives fiction a crucial position; it is a matter of life and death. If the women cannot convince, influence, hypnotize, or spell the prince/Walser, they and other women will die. In Fevvers' situation, if she cannot put a spell on Walser, he will turn her into a humbug, or in other words, he will turn her into his idea of woman. The root of literature, storytelling takes the form of a magic spell. In *The Thousand and One Nights*, storytelling also functions as a medium to create love between the teller and the listener; the stories enchant the prince by giving pleasure which eventually teaches him love. During the nights he spends with the two sisters, the prince goes through a process at the end of which he is purified of his hatred for women and able to love them. Similarly, Fevvers as the modern Scheherazade tells her own story calling it an autobiography and enchants Walser with Liz in place of the sister, Dünyazad (57). Walser is enchanted by the unbelievable things they narrate without having the courage to question them although it was initially Walser who came to trick Fevvers to make her give away her secret. Instead, he is tricked into believing her story, which recalls the failure of the prince's plan to kill Scheherazade in the morning. This allusion to *The Thousand and One Nights* suggests that the art of story telling is a strategy that women can use to overturn the patriarchal power by using language as a magic spell. The women prevent the men's aggression and trap them in their stories or fiction. Here, language or fiction becomes a medium to produce change in subjectivity and in relationships.

Fevvers' co-narrative with Liz in the first section carries many aspects of oral tradition. In *Negotiating with the Dead*, Atwood mentions an important feature of the performance which is that the song or the story cannot be separated from the time of performing since it is in the performance, in the confrontation with the audience that the story is created and recreated. This process requires the poet to take into consideration the audience's reaction since the physical encounter with the audience makes it necessary for the singer to appeal to the audience's expectations. Even the continuation of the performance depends on the poet's success at satisfying the audience since the audience may interrupt, or even stop listening if they do not like the story (Atwood 2002, 48 -49). In this sense, Fevvers and Liz's narrative is very much similar to oral tradition. Like the poets of ancient times, they adjust their story according to Walser's reactions, use body language and vocal effects to give the desired effect, and the continuation of their performance depends on their success at captivating Walser in their performance, in which they succeed. Under the spell of Fevvers' story in the room with the smell, the "essence of Fevvers," the champagne and the tea that he is offered, and Fevvers' batting her eyelashes, he cannot leave the room, for as he himself realizes, he is not "allowed" to (52). Micheal also mentions that Fevvers disassociates story telling from its phallic power by not using a pen (Michael 1994, 513). I would add that what stands against phallic power is the allusion to oral tradition itself because oral tradition- lullabies, fairy-tales, elegies especially in Turkish culture—usually connotes women. Oral tradition recalls the image of grandmothers telling fairy-tales to children, mothers singing lullabies, or women singing mournful songs at funerals. This is not to suggest that men are outside this tradition. Of course, there are the troubadours in Medieval Europe, aşıks (travelling poets) like Karacaoğlan in Anatolia, but the point is that when compared to the print-age, oral tradition is more welcoming to women as subject of their songs, poems, and tales. Therefore, I will suggest that allusion to oral tradition is part of Carter's challenge to the objectification of woman in language and literature.

In the first section, even though it is written in the third person narration, the reader is identified with Walser, which is also noted by Kérchy and Boehm (Kérchy 2004, 118; Boehm 1995, 6). The third person narration mirrors Walser's point of view. While listening to her story, Walser debates with himself the plausibility of her story, draws logical conclusions, suspects, and looks for the contradictions in the narrative just as the reader does. With Walser, we try to understand who or what Fevvers is and after the first section, we decide to follow Fevvers in the circus. In addition to occupying the position of the writer, Fevvers also becomes the art object with Walser in the place of the reader because the story is Fevvers' life story and about her identity. Fevvers' narration with

Liz's contribution is a fairy-tale-like one encouraging the reader as well as Walser to suspect her identity. What she tells about herself—her being left in a basket at the door of a brothel, being raised by the women and adopted especially by Lizzie, her feathers coming out at puberty, her adventures—creates doubts about her reality; what she tells is unbelievable, yet she is so sure of herself that she challenges Walser/the reader by giving both checkable and uncheckable names as proofs- the referred people are real but what she tells about them makes it impossible for Walser to go check whether they are true or not. The question at stake, "Is she fact or fiction" applies to Fevvers' identity, woman who is presented as an art object. By employing a woman's body as a work of art, Carter reveals that woman is an artificial construct that is objectified by the male gaze whose desire for the mother turns woman into a fantasized maternal body to whom he does not allow a subjectivity.

The novel's motto, *"seeing is believing",* comes as an answer to the question of "fact or fiction" (15). *NC* suggests that Fevvers is a work of art whose secret lies not in what the public or Walser wants to learn, that is, whether she is a fact or fiction, but in the "suspension of disbelief" and the success of art is contingent on *fooling* the reader/viewer (17). *Seeing is believing* suggests that illusion is the foundation of our perception of reality. When it is remembered that Fevvers owes her identity to her ability to fool the reader/viewer, her secret becomes her mastery of creating illusion. The motto, *seeing is believing,* points to the dominance of sight in producing belief as an answer to whether Fevvers, woman, is fact or fiction. What creates Fevvers, woman, is the gaze; the tyranny of the male gaze (of Freud for instance) that sees 'a nothing to see' in the female sex and concludes that this 'nothing to see' must desire to possess what he has, for otherwise he will have to recognize difference and accept that he is not the norm (*Speculum*, 47- 48). Then, since Fevvers does not let the gaze see whether she has *it* or not, whether she is fact or fiction, she has wings or not, she is resisting to be sent back to the void of language whose binary logic will deprive her of her pleasure.

Aggression by applying rationality, scientific method as Walser does on Fevvers' different body is an example of the male aggression on sexual difference. Walser wants to turn her back into the idea of woman and put an end to her desire, her pleasure which is expressed in her resistance to definition. Since Fevvers does not allow anyone to define her within the binary logic that appropriates silence to her, and places her as lack, the negative of the male subject, there appears the possibility of a different configuration of female subjectivity. Fevvers symbolizes the potential female subject that can find herself a home, a language that will not repress her pleasure.

Language's crucial role in the capture of women in representation is manifested in Fevvers' fear on hearing Mr. Rosencreutz call her by her first name Sophia. His act of exposing his knowledge of her legal name heralds the danger she is in. Fevvers expresses that "it is as if it put [her] in his power, that he should know [her] name..." (81). Naming is defining, entrapping in the definition, thus exercising power by confiscating the other, the different in his own idea/ideology. It is the magical power that enables the dragons in the Earth Sea who speak the language that consists of the names of everything control human beings and animals. Fevvers' panic at hearing her name reveals her secret—that her power is grounded in creating the "Fevvers," a winged woman, a mystery for the public while Sophia, her first name is reserved only for those who will not impose their will on her. In the Earth Sea, confiding one's name to another is an act of mutual confidence, sign of trust (Le Guin 1993). Similarly, Fevvers is disturbed when she realizes that Mr Rosencreutz knows her real name. Knowing her real name or defining her means having power over her so he confides her name in those whom she trusts, Liz, for instance. Like Ursula K. Le Guin, Carter reveals the magical power of language; it can create, control, and produce subjects. Representation, narration is both the prison and the door out of it. When Fevvers chooses names like the Cockney Venus, Helen of the High Wire, and the Virgin Whore for herself, she places herself out of the male fantasy and indulges in her own desire by jamming the binary oppositions; the mechanism that bereaves her sexuality, her difference, pleasure. She plays with the art of naming by choosing many controversial names in order to hide her real name or identity.

Carter suggests that reality is an illusion that we believe in: she proposes reality as belief. From the luxury of Ma Nelson's brothel to the shaman's spirits, this motto provides the reader with the criteria to test what is real and what is not, which equates reality with belief. Fiction, then, is real as long as you believe in it. With the motto, *seeing is believing*, Carter extends the ground of Fevvers' reality to all narrations in the novel. When discussing the multiple narratives in *NC*, Finney proposes that Carter depicts fictional worlds and realistic depictions one after another—such as the luxury of the brothel that is destroyed with the daylight and its burning down; Madame Schreck and her evaporation—to suggest that a balance between fact and fiction is needed to be maintained since fact alone fails to convey the human experience while fiction is doomed to end when the narration is over (Finney 1998, 167). I agree with the statement that Carter explores what fiction means for human experience; yet, I would suggest that rather than pointing out to the temporality of fiction and its necessary end when exposed to the factual, the reason why Carter brings together extraordinary, shocking, strange accounts together with the realistic accounts of London, for instance, is to show that fiction is the underlying structure of the factual. What Carter exposes is, in Irigaray's terminology, the underlying imaginary of the symbolic. That is to say, Carter reveals the mythology, ideology, and desires that govern life, our actions, and institutions like the brothel and the museum of woman monsters, but since Carter takes them to their logical conclusions, they seem unrealistic. Woman for example is not much different from the monster in the logic of identity. What grounds the factual is fiction; it only sounds extraordinary and unreal, because the facts are taken to extreme ends and shown without veils. *NC* is both realistic and fantastic in the sense that Carter exposes the fantasies that create reality. In addition, and this is what makes the novel a narrative of possibilities and change, she indulges in distorting this mythology to serve her quest for change. By revealing to what extent fiction and phantasy can shape our perception of the world and our relationships, she suggests that change can again be brought about through fiction, or fantasy.

Carter presents illusion as fiction, or art, which produce beliefs and shape reality: *seeing is believing*. Illusion is what, how, where, why, when we see or cannot or do not see. Despite the (male) gaze's claim to authority, the objectivity and capability of the pair of eyes cannot be taken as granted. First of all, there are limits to the reliability of the biological eye. Science says that there are no colours in the world; it is the play of light and the interaction of the cornea and light that gives us the illusion of a colourful world. Also, the biological eye does not work the same way in all the living things: bulls for example are colour blind and dogs see the world white and black whereas snakes can see the infrared that we cannot see. Besides the biological limits, the perception of the eye and reason clash. Optical illusions, for instance, show that it is impossible to count on your eyes since what the eye sees and logic says are not always the same thing.

In addition to the illusion created by the biological eye and the play of lights, the human mind can create *optical* illusions on purpose, which is called art. The art of photography, for example, thanks to developing technologies makes the distinction between the original, real image and the produced image difficult to see. By distorting the images on the computer, with photoshop for instance, the original images can gain a different meaning. Also like the eye, the camera has a certain angle and space in which it can see and include an object in a square. Furthermore, it is the human mind which is a complex of ideology that chooses what and from what angle to see and fix into the square of the photograph. Taking the picture of a naked woman looking into the mirror is one thing and including for example the photographer's hand in the same square is another.

In cinema, films through various techniques like repetitious images throughout the film, or split screen produce an interpretation of reality. In *Requiem for a Dream,* for instance, Aronofsky shows Harry's desperate dependence on drugs and the way he clings to them, in the same screen with his mother, Sara, who is clinging to antidepressants. In the same screen, we view the two desperate people clutching their pills and think that after all there is no difference between using drugs and taking anti-depressants and watching TV, which can all be interpreted as a vain attempt to fill the gap that one feels. These examples warn us not to take the *eye* and the act of seeing as something innocent or objective and make us *see* that seeing is an intelligent, creative, political activity that gives meaning to what is *seen.*

When Carter presents witchcraft as illusion and art, Liz, the witch, also comes to signify the writer. First of all, her accompanying Fevvers aims at guiding, helping, and providing feedback to Fevvers, the woman. In this sense, she *hatches* Fevvers by instructing her on what woman is in society or how she must protect herself. Her famous power over time is the power of her fiction. In the dressing room in the first chapter, it is thanks to Liz's control of time that Walser is tied hand and foot to Fevvers' story. Then, her rescuing Fevvers in a toy train from the Grand Duke's palace is the power of her fiction over that of the Duke's. It is significant that Liz loses her handbag and Ma Nelson's heritage, the father time, in "Siberia" when the narration goes haywire and the woman writer is in perplexity by the question of how to end *NC*. The woman writer or Liz cannot control her fiction because the genre dictates marriage for the ending but this ending means going back to male economy of desire. The rejection of the male economy of desire causes disturbance and both the woman writer and Fevvers go hysterical in this desperate situation. What hysteria will produce is a question and there is nothing to do but "let the event dictate themselves" as Fevvers desperately murmurs (245). The loss of the father clock, Liz's power over fiction, echoes the woman writer's uncomfortable position and her lack of a genre and an ending, a model for her female subject in the domain of literature.

Walser's re-entry into the symbolic and into society after the amnesia in the tribe illustrates how language and identity are acquired within a given a society. Having lost his memory, and the mythological and ideological package with it, he regains his identity. He opens his eyes with touch, "the first language," when Olga kisses him. Then the very first thing Walser learns is how to get food, that is by rubbing his stomach, which signifies the body and the bodily needs as the foundation of the knowledge of the others and of our relation to the others. The first relation to the world is through the bodily needs and love is the foundation of this knowledge. In a way, Olga mothers him and the shaman fathers him by introducing him into the social structure that he must fit into through language acquisition. Yet, the individual is not a *tabula rasa*; in Walser's case, he has scraps in his memory of his previous life. When Walser feels uncomfortable with the shaman's interpretation of his memories in accord with his own religious system, we observe the clash of language and the individual's sensations and feelings. The language that the individual has to express his/her feelings, sensations in is not a transparent tool. Instead, language selects, limits, interprets, and thus translates these sensations into something else. This is how socialization is completed; Walser's sensations are translated into the shaman's religion and thereby he is appropriated into this society as an apprentice shaman. By referring to the villagers' conception of the world as "a common dream" that "should rather be called an 'idea' than a dream," Carter suggests that what we believe to be reality is actually the order and categorization of knowledge that we constitute in language (253).

NC is full of changes and potentials for change that desire can initiate. Change appears in Walser, in the panopticon, and in Mignon. In these transformations, Carter reveals desire as the initiative of change that can produce a new language. Walser starts his adventures upon his desire for Fevvers and this adventure ends up with drafting an autobiography. Mignon, who first enters the narration in the role of the victim woman, turns out to be a lesbian with the magic spell of a combination of music and desire. Mignon finds her language when she starts to sing and pairs up with the Princess who plays the piano for the tigers.

The connection between desire and change is most evident in the advent of the female utopia upon the escape from the House of Correction in which female victims are imprisoned under inhumanly conditions. What brings about the change in the panopticon is female desire that touch awakens although language and even the look is forbidden among the wardresses and the prisoners. These women use the taboo bodily liquids like menstrual and venial blood, which are the symbols of female sexuality and they can be regarded as *object a* that remains as residue in the logic of identity, together with excrement that belongs to the anal economy that governs the male imaginary in order to write their language that frees them (*Speculum* 74 -75). What Carter suggests here is the need for a language that can represent sexual difference and female pleasure. This new writing recognizes and represents woman's body allowing the women to relate to their own bodies and desires. Discovering their pleasure, the wardresses and the prisoners flee from the panopticon, which comes as a shock to the countess. The Countess correctly ponders: "Were they not forbidden discourse with the inmates? Did not the forbidden thing itself forbid?" (217). Yet, desire, even when the look is forbidden—maybe because the look is forbidden since the epistemology which is founded on the male gaze that cannot see the female genitals does not allow woman express her desire—breaks free and induces the women to write their language on "a blank sheet of fresh paper on which they could inscribe whatever future they wished" (218). Nevertheless, Carter does not pursue this idea. Through Liz's comment on the fate of the male babies, Carter suggests that freedom will not be born in a non-male society because simply there are men and women in the world and what is needed is sexual difference which requires the existence of two sexes. Carter is careful and wise enough not to offer a utopia. Utopia is the nowhere and if it becomes somewhere, it will no more be utopia. This is because stabilization and definition belong to the existing epistemology that is grounded on the metaphysics of presence. The female desire and her utopia need a language that will not need to stabilize and define to know. It is always in the future but this future guides the present.

By showing how narration, illusion, and witchcraft come together, Carter proposes that there is no such distinction between fact and fiction. As subjects are the constructions in the play of the subject-object dichotomy governed by the law of the phallus, the reality that is produced by these fictive females and males cannot be other than fiction. What is defined as woman is the fantasy of the male who dwells in the ideal maternal. This is a novel on epistemology and an account of what a piece of work man and woman is—to borrow the repeated allusion to *Hamlet* in *NC*. Carter never lets the reader forget that what s/he is reading is fiction through the frequent use of allusions to literary criticism and other literary works. The allusion to Shakespeare quoted first by Fevvers to nudge Walser/the reader that she is constructing her life, identity in language is quoted by Walser twice at significant moments: first, when he encounters difference in the monkeys' lesson for the first time and then under the influence of hallucinogenic urine in Siberia (111; 238). At these moments, he realizes how vulnerable, ironic the security, consistency of our sense of identity that language lures us into is.

When fiction has that much power, it can be a tool to produce change as well, and *NC* is a novel full of possibilities of change that is reflected in the transformations that many characters go through besides the change of setting, and narrator. In this narrative we are also invited into "the freedom to juggle with being, and, indeed, with the language which is vital to our being, that lies at the heart of burlesque" (103). The picaresque structure of *NC* that advances towards a catastrophe parallels a similar change in narration in the last section. The narrative voice starts to fluctuate: point of view, the position of the reader and the writer together with the art object start to shift and make it difficult to decide who is "the butt of the joke" (295). Following are the concluding remarks on the significance of the changes in narration and how these shifts relate to Carter's discussion on art and criticism of language.

As mentioned before, the first section of *NC* is written in the third person narration from Walser's point of view whereby the reader identifies with Walser. The third person narration continues in the second section titled "St Petersburg," but this time, the narrator steps in like the baboushka who opens the section in a fairy-tale fashion: "There was a pig" (95). The baboushka also hints that the tale will not continue in a traditional way by finishing her tale abruptly in the second sentence of her tale: "Wolf eat him" upon Little Ivan's prompting her (97). When Walser is writing his description of St Petersburg on his typewriter, the narrator intervenes: "*St Petersburg, a city built of hubris, imagination and desire...*" [Walser's narration]. "As we are, ourselves; or as we ought to be [the narrator]" (97).

And the narrator also psychoanalyzes the clowns when they produce items like lavatory paper that symbolize the anal imaginary: "(Anality, the one quality that indeed they shared with children)" (124). In this section, the previous reader, Walser turns into a writer, a journalist who is writing about Fevvers and the circus. Yet, the narrator turns him into the object of art at the same time with the comments on Walser's writing and also by writing about him with a scientific distance. In the sixth chapter, the narrator analyzes his thoughts about Fevvers and Liz and his state of mind with a scientific clarity and brevity. Besides, the narrator identifies Fevvers with Walser when Fevvers gets entrapped in the Grand Duke's palace which signifies Fevvers' entrapment in the male fiction that turns her into *objects d'art* (187): "And she [Fevvers] felt more and more vague, less and less her own mistress. Walser would have recognized the sensation which gripped her; he had felt much the same in her dressing-room at the Alhambra, when midnight struck the third time" (190). The Grand Duke's power over Fevvers corresponds to his fiction of woman that apprehends Fevvers. In this section, the narrator becomes more active and reminds the reader of significant details in a friendly manner. Yet,

instead of these details, these comments remind the reader of the
fictionality of what s/he is reading:

> this Sleeping Beauty of a city [...] yearning to burst through the present
> into the violence of that authentic history to which this narrative-as must
> by now be obvious! – does not belong (97).
>
> let me tell you something about Fevvers, if you haven't noticed
> it for yourself already; she is a girl of philosophical bent (185).

This feature also appears in Fevvers and Liz's narration in the
first section of the novel, so it is possible to identify these women with the
narrator. Fevvers says: "And so the first chapter of my life went up in
flames, sir" (50). "'Fevvers," we named her, and so she will be till the end
of the chapter, [...]" says Liz (13). The next section, "Siberia," opens with
Fevvers' first-person narration and oscillates between Fevvers and the
third person throughout the section mirroring the strange atmosphere of
Siberia, the events, and people that are narrated. It seems that the narrator
has joined the chaos in this section: the strange opening of the third
chapter hints that the narrator can be a bit lost in Siberia as well:

> Although *no signpost* points the way there and *even the track*
> made by the shackled feet of its inhabitants in the course of the dolorous
> journey to the place is soon *obscured* by the rapid summer growth of the
> mosses and small plants or erased by winter's snow so that no trace
> remains of their arrivals, we are in the vicinity of the settlement of R
> (210, italics mine).

The narrator babbles that there is no way to know where *we* are
but it reassures us that *we* are *there*. We start to feel a bit hysterical as
well. In this section also starts a debate between Fevvers and Liz (197 -
198; 279 -286), Liz and the escapee (239 -240), the outlaws and Fevvers
(229-230) on the issues and themes that have been implied in the previous
two chapters. In the first chapter, Liz and Fevvers discuss their situation
and meanwhile, they give away their secrets—that Fevvers is mimicking
and they are supporting the struggle financially. The fate of the new
woman but more significantly or together with this issue, the ending of the
novel itself is what is at stake in these discussions. The alternatives for

Fevvers and Liz are thus: the female Quixote and Sancha Panza may join the female utopia but there is the question of male babies; they may join the outlaws but the outlaws like women better absent (230) and so Liz decides they should vanish in the storm with the clowns' death dance; they may join the Colonel and continue supporting the struggle but mimicry gives emergency signals because it is adopted too long; and of course there is the happy ending though in a slightly perverted version: "the trapeze artiste who rescues the clown," which is approached with irony or rather mockery since in the year of the publication of *NC*, 1984, women have long abandoned their faith in sweet homes (281).

In her comprehensive reading of *NC*, Kérchy argues that Fevvers' suggestions for the novel's ending reflect the woman writer's ironic look at her place in male-dominated literature in which her subjectivity is already constructed on the male idea of feminity and her "deconstructive feminist gesture" to subvert the representation of feminity (Kérchy 2004, 111-112). Liz's ironic remarks on the happy endings certainly illustrate Kérchy's argument. In this section the text becomes hysterical just like Fevvers. Kérchy argues that the whole text shows the symptoms of hysteria but I would suggest that the first two sections of the novel reflect mimicry like Fevvers in that the narration is consistent while giving away its fictionality, and then in the last section titled "Siberia" the text and woman writer becomes hysterical because they confront the conflict with the boundaries of literature (Kérchy 2004, 112 -114). The narrator changes abruptly and Fevvers and Liz are at a loss about how to end their story as well as they are lost in Siberia.

The discussion between Fevvers and Liz is mostly about what to do with Walser, the man, at the end of the novel. While Liz is for discarding him from their story, from the story of woman, Fevvers cannot dispense with him. Her touching beseeching Liz to give Walser a chance deserves a large space:

> "An *amanuensis*," she said to Lizzie. And not of my trajectory, alone, but of yours, too, Lizzie; of your long history of exile and cunning which *you've scarcely hinted to him*, which will fill up ten times more of his notebooks than *my story* ever did. Think of him as the amanuensis of all those whose tales *we*'ve yet to tell him, the *histories of those woman* who would otherwise go down nameless and forgotten, erased from history as

if they had never been, so that he, too, will put his poor shoulder to the wheel and help to give the world a little turn into the new era that begins tomorrow (285, italics mine).

Here the position of the writer and the reader shift again: this time Liz becomes the writer and Fevvers the reader and/or an active participant art object. It is as if Liz is the author of *NC*, Angela Carter since it is she who has compacted the "long history of exile and cunning" of woman, of Mignon, the Princess, the Sleeping Beauty, Olga, Fanny, Cobwebs etc. Fevvers here becomes the reader discussing with the author and pleading her not to dismiss Walser, the man from the novel. Whether to dismiss man from the novel is actually the question of whether there is any hope in the future, whether there can ever be the possibility of an existence for woman in a world with man, whether man can ever let the other, woman, be and live her pleasure.

Fevvers has faith in man, or more correctly in man's contribution to language and fiction. She talks of him as an amanuensis, a writer who can listen and write the "histories of those woman" without imposing his idea of woman on them, who can let woman speak for herself, speak her pleasure. The writer/Liz is not very comfortable with the idea of man's contribution to this history; nevertheless she "looked on him kindly" since there is woman's desire for him (293). In addition to Fevvers' identification with the reader and the writer, she also occupies the place of art object in these discussions since this novel is about her identity and life. Then, Carter once more, in a bolder manner, destabilizes the hierarchies in literature and language. Liz, as the writer of the book about Fevvers discusses, negotiates about what to write about her, and in the end, she even obeys Fevvers' desire to unite with Walser even though she dislikes this ending. She allows the art object to participate in the decision about her fate just like Orhan Pamuk does in *My Name is Red* in which horses in the pictures, the colours, narrate us their stories. This is a subversive move in a literary tradition that produces truths in an order which is determined by subject-object dichotomies. Yet, within these dichotomies, the orders are so *fantastic* that hysteria can play havoc with them in *fantasy*, as Carter does in this section.

The catastrophic atmosphere in this section ends with a long wrestling that takes place in the god-hut of the village in the dark in which there is no way to know who is wrestling with whom. This wrestling ends with the entrance of the inhabitants/audience/the reader (?) into the scene. Fevvers manages to fuel herself with "the wind of wonder" from the inhabitants, which shows that this is not the end of the *ludic mimicry* (290). She curtseys like a performer and bats her eyelashes at Walser as she did in the dressing room in the first section (291). The last section titled "Envoi" again identifies the reader with Walser by opening with Fevvers' confessions on the tricks they played on Walser/the reader who is actually no more interested in the reliability of the narrator, the plausibility of narration or "in the mood to draw any definite conclusions from this fact" (292). The change in Walser, the reader, man is reflected in his babbling and this babbling is an *autobiography*; it is no more about Fevvers/woman. Walser "contemplate[s], as in a mirror, the self he was so busily reconstructing" and his first trial that starts with a confidant "I" and introduces Fevvers as his wife is interrupted by Fevvers, upon which Walser "took himself apart and put himself together" in language. This time, his tale is composed of

> Jack, ever an adventurous boy, ran away with the circus for the sake of a bottle blonde [...] He got himself [...] an apprenticeship in the higher form of the confidence trick, initiated by a wily old pederast who bamboozled him completely. [...] And now, hatched out of the shell of unknowing by a combination of a blow on the head and a sharp spasm of erotic ecstasy, I shall have to start all over gain (294).

The pronouns in his narrative start to shift and collapse: first he becomes the third person "an adventurous boy" (294), then he picks up the "I." His commencement in devising a language, especially his awareness of the artful nature of pronouns is promising, yet the question of what he will produce, what will become of the new man and the new woman hangs in the air that vibrates with the potentiality of Fevvers' laughter.

Yet, bringing about the union of lovers at the end is a sort of confession that the woman writer has not liberated her fiction from the constrictions of the literary heritage. And, yet, again—since the reader has that much right to be a bit hysterical as well since s/he is also tempted into hysteria in such a closing chapter, or, to be fair, actually, it was the reader who used free will (?) "to spend a few nights at the circus" (91)—there is hope in the *confidence trick* that will continue to trick and tickle the minds but what it will produce is not knowable.

CHAPTER TWO

THE BLIND ASSASSIN

2.1. The Con/Fusion of Love and Hatred

In *BA*, through the family history narrated by Iris along with the inner story told by the third person narrator, Atwood exposes how patriarchal culture maintains men's dominance over women by reducing them to maternal function on which the male constructs its identity. The story of the two sisters, Laura and Iris, bears witness to reduction of women to silence that perpetuates the dominance of male values, and deprives women of subjective identity for them to become active participants in society. Representing women in maternal function and appropriating the female as the absence in language for the construction of meaning for the male to assert his truth, his value leaves women in a status in which they become an object to be exchanged among men. Finding themselves as object to the male desire and in a silence about their relation to their mothers and to themselves as women, women encounter the difficulty in understanding their identity as separate from their mothers and other women.

Since this economy of representation does not provide the conditions for women to differentiate from the mother, women get entrapped in the maternal function in which they exist to nourish men, guard their houses and names while they are left in a problematic relationship to themselves and other women. Although the desire of/for the mother is the subject's first attachment to itself and to others, and "[t]ouch comes before sight, before speech [;] [i]t is the first language and the last, and it always tells the truth" as the narrator states, the construction of language does not let any representation, appropriation of this first desire for women and thereby women get struck in this wordless desire (311).⁹ The two sisters'

---

⁹ References to *BA* will be given as page numbers in parenthesis hereafter.

painful way of becoming women in *BA* can be read as Irigaray's critique of patriarchal society put into fiction; the silenced desire for/of the mother as the foundation of society, women as objects of exchange, and a destructive world as a result. The destructive relationship between Iris and Laura is what Carter avoids by not placing Liz and Fevvers in a family in *NC*. In *BA*, Atwood demonstrates the consequences of *becoming a woman* in the family, which is the problematic relationships among women and between women and men.

The question of female identity in relation to the social order and representation is introduced on the very first page of the novel that informs of Laura's suicide. Laura's death is connected to the war, the news comes from a policeman, and Iris, her sister is needed to identify her:

> Ten days after the war ended, my sister Laura drove a car off a bridge [...]. Nothing much was left of her but charred smithereens.
> I was informed of the accident by a policeman: the car was mine, and they'd traced the licence. His tone was respectful: no doubt he recognized Richard's name.
> [...]
> "I suppose you want someone to identify her," I said (3).

The basic concerns that will be elaborated in the novel are implied here: the mention of the war puts the question of female identity that emerges with the need to "identify" Laura's body in relation to the social order, and the involvement of the police and the respect that Richard's name arises in the police furthers this implication by adding a representative of state authority that respects a patriarch. With the mention of the licence ownership becomes part of the issue and meanwhile, it places suspicion on Iris as the owner of the car. Hereafter, the "inquest" starts to weave together these clues in order to "identify" Laura, woman (4). Hence, the whole novel can be read as the identification of woman in patriarchal culture.

The fact that female identity is called on question upon the death of a woman, her *real* absence, is significant. This implies that the representation of woman as absence in language and the other in subject constitution consigns women to oblivion leaving 'charred smithereens' through which women have to perceive themselves and each other. The real absence of Laura, that is her death, necessitates the investigation of the operations of absence and presence on Iris. Therefore, Iris' identification of her sister, Laura, with the fragments left from her body signifies the undertaking to divulge the problematic representation of women, which is entangled with the representation of mothers. In the shock of the news, the memory of Reenie arises in Iris' mind:

> What I remembered then was Reenie, from when we were little. It was Reenie who'd done the bandaging, of scrapes and cuts and minor injuries: Mother might be resting, or doing good deeds elsewhere, but Reenie was always there. She'd […] give us a lump of brown sugar to get us close our mouths (4-5).

Iris' trouble with her identity manifests itself in her remembering Reenie as a mother substitution who bandages wounds and nourishes in the absence of her mother. This memory shows that Reenie fulfills the maternal function on the level of need for Iris. Reenie's association with the absence of her mother points out to the representation of the mother in the constitution of male subject as absence and thereby delegating it as the other of his identity that holds up the presence end. What Iris needs is the absence, the mother, the mother-substitution when she learns that Laura is dead. This trouble about her identity, the problematic construction of the mother that stems from the lack of representation of mother-daughter relationship, explains her part in Laura's suicide that was implicit in the mention of the ownership of the licence.

That Iris searches for what is lost looking at the picture of Laura on the factory picnic evinces that she is trying to realize, understand, and find a way to represent her loss of Laura and also her mother. Laura's absence becomes Laura's presence. Without a representation, symbolization of separation from the mother, women get lost as subjects and now, Laura's death, her absence in life, drives Iris to see her sister as a separate subject "beyond her own reflection" (8). Iris is searching for her sister who was lost in Iris' reflection when she was alive as if Laura was herself and now that Laura is not in life to reflect Iris to herself, that is the same as herself, Iris must find her sister, which means undertaking the difficult task of realizing Laura and herself as different individuals in a culture where all women occupy the same position as mothers.

Starting with Laura's suicide, Iris in her old age goes back in time to their childhood that sheds light on how Laura lost hold of life at the age of twenty-five, and her own part in this event. Aware of her complicity in the destruction of Laura, she narrates how she has become both the victim and victimizer in a social order that makes these terms impossible to apply to women as women become nothing other than commodities in the market to be exchanged among men. The story is a tragic one for both sisters who get trapped in the male desire, that of Alex and Richard, that feeds on woman by appropriating women to maternal role. The result is that Iris submits to the demands of male values accepting the feminine role and cannot differentiate from her mother, and Laura on the other hand destroys herself rejecting the feminine role in the material world.

Constraining women in the maternal role to maintain male identity and values leaves women in confusion as to their relationship to the mother and the sister. As an elder sister, Iris finds herself in a complicated relation to her younger sister and mother. The fact that all women are mothers in male representation economy requires Iris to act the maternal role, which makes it impossible for her to understand her relation to her mother and her sister. The only way to express her love for the mother is to take up the same role; she is helpful with Laura playing the role of the mother when Laura is a baby in order to be close to her mother. Mothering Laura, becoming a mother is the only way to express her desire for the mother and to be with her mother in her deathbed. In such a puzzling position, it is only natural that the subject of desire mingles with the object of desire and Iris cannot differentiate herself from the mother and then, Laura becomes herself (Iris) and thus Iris remains in a problematic relation to both Laura in the place of herself and to herself in the place of her mother. Iris cannot love her mother as a separate subject from herself and in return, she cannot love herself as the subject of her desire different from her mother. As Irigaray states, the non-representation of mother-daughter relationships makes love a complicated matter between women (*An Ethics*, 87).

Being at a loss as to her role and identity as an elder sister, Iris confuses herself with Laura. This confusion about her identity as a separate entity from her sister, Laura, and her rebellion against the forced maternal role on her show itself in the form of aggression towards Laura, which is actually her aggression towards herself since in the maternal game that she is induced to Laura becomes herself. The desire for the mother finds expression in Iris' competition for the only place in the mother which is the only place allocated to women *to be* and to love (themselves and other women) (*An Ethics*, 86 -87). Iris competes for this unique place which is the only way to express love for the mother and resents the demanding role of maternity that is required from her when she was a child herself: "I felt I was the victim of an injustice: why was it always me who was supposed to be a good sister to Laura, instead of the other way around? Surely my mother loved Laura more than she loved me" (116). Her bitterness for being compelled to be a mother to Laura which is worded as being a good sister invokes aggressiveness towards Laura. The childish behavior like hiding from Laura when she is looking for her or frightening her when she takes her envelopes by saying that the glue on the envelopes is made from horses are the expressions of her disagreement with her role (117).

When the mother dies, Iris finds herself in a worse situation since now she occupies the place of the mother who she thinks abandons her all of a sudden. Taking her mother's death as betrayal, now she starts to take revenge from Laura. After Liliana's funeral, her anger goes as far as pushing Laura off the pond just because Laura believes the story of the mother's death, which is that she is in heaven. This is Iris' first attack on Laura or on herself as she reflects herself on Laura when Liliana's death leaves Iris in the place of the incomprehensible absence and Laura in the place of the daughter/herself.

Laura's response to her mother's death differs from that of Iris. As a child, Laura takes God and language seriously rather than registering the metaphor. When the schoolteacher says that God is everywhere, she is frightened by the possibility of God appearing anywhere in the house. Yet, after her mother's death, she seeks relief in the idea of God as a metaphor for the union with the mother, to fill the gap, the irretrievable loss. The idea of union with God, the desired and impossible union that Sufis, Buddhists, mystics strive for; the union with a deity to replace the lost union with the mother, derives its strength and perpetuation in the non-representation of the desire for the forbidden mother. Instead of replacing the mother by adopting the maternal role, Laura invests in the domain of religion, God as a substitute for her desire for a union with the mother.

Her relation to God which is the foundation of identity in a society put her in a problematic position. Her rejection of her role as a mother-woman makes it impossible for her to survive in a society that does not recognize women as other than mothers of men. She resembles her mother, Liliana in that as a teenager, she devotes herself to charity like soothing the poor by offering her services at the soup- kitchen. Instead of the reflections of God on earth like the father (yet, interestingly she confuses her father with God when he walks in the turret) or Richard, she chooses the god itself for fulfillment of her desire (168). While Iris is pushed to the materialist end contending herself with expensive items of clothing for instance, Laura follows Liliana's path in her idealism and contempt of the flesh. Thus, unlike Liz and Fevvers in *NC*, the sisters cannot love each other as individual women when they are stuck in the maternal role in the patriarchal family.

Since patriarchal culture is based on the father-son relationship to ensure its perpetuation by the transmission of property from father to son, the Chase family is in danger of dissipation with only daughters who will abandon the family for another man's house. Up to Liliana's death, the father, Norval, neglects his daughters since they will be no use for The Chase and Sons factories, but upon this death as it puts an end to the hope for a son to continue his name and his business, he realizes that he is obliged to content himself with Iris and he starts teaching Iris accounting. Yet, his attempt to teach Iris basic principles in commerce ends in vain since Iris, having no interest and agency in this commerce as a woman, is confounded with the numbers in the account book as she is already at a loss about her identity in relation to the other women in the family. Irigaray interprets the difficulty in mathematics as the symptom of a lack of a representation for women to count the mothers, sisters, themselves in the family when all women occupy the same position (*Speculum* 45 -46). When Iris reaches puberty, Norval gives up his endeavor to turn Iris into a son; nevertheless, he discovers another opportunity to make use of Iris when he meets Richard, the new money who needs an old, aristocratic name to raise him in society. During the depression years, Richard appears as a saviour to Norval who is now at a short move from bankruptcy.

The factory picnic when the factory is burned down and Alex and Richard both make their entry into the sisters' life is a milestone in their life. The dinner scene gives clues about the turn their life will take afterwards and about each of the sisters' way of dealing with others. Laura sabotages this arrangement by inviting Alex to dinner which is actually given for Richard who is probably assessing Norval's assets which include Iris as well. Iris' blindness to the circumstances due to her competition with Laura in attaining the love of her mother, directs her attention towards Alex who catches her attention when she realizes Laura's interest in him. She shows care in arranging the seating plan safely seating Laura far from Alex and herself next to him. Although Reenie makes a lot of effort with the dinner consulting Adelia's cookbook, the food is a disappointment since the aristocratic values that Adelia represents are being replaced by another set of values, namely that of the middle-class. This failure foreshadows the fruitlessness of Norval's hope in the future of his business and family with Richard's intervention as the representative of new money that the father needs to keep his factories open.

After the upheaval when the factory is burned down, Laura and Iris become alibis in hiding Alex, the suspect, in the attic and this prefigures Alex's later secret and complicated relationship with them. When the sisters are harboring Alex, they become alibis against the state and Richard who immediately accuses Alex of burning the factory. This alliance brings the sisters closer as Robinson also notes (Robinson 354). They share the maternal role by nourishing and then send Alex to the world. Afterwards, they will be defined by Alex on the axis of material and spiritual dichotomy; Iris ministers his bodily needs in the role of Martha and Laura functions as the guardian of his being spiritually acting the Mary part in Christ/Alex's identity. They become subject to the male's spiritual and physical needs as Iris realizes in her old age (264).

Laura's awareness of her and her sister's position in a world dominated by men is manifest in her recreating the picture of herself, Iris, and Alex on the factory picnic. Laura produces two pictures by cutting off the picture to include one of the sisters with Alex with the other sister's hand on the corner. These pictures show that men are separating the sisters, and with a man between them they reject each other. In this picture, the man, Alex, becomes the main signifier, the phallus that orders the economy of desire in which women have no means to relate to each other; man prevents the sisters from loving each other. The photograph also alludes to Genesis with the apple tree, a man and a woman whose other is absent. Although in Genesis, Eve is accepted as the only woman, some interpretations propose that there was another woman before Eve called Lilith who is cursed by God as she refused to obey Adam and adopt an inferior status and escaped from him. Lilith and Eve are the first pair of women in history who cannot come together as a result of the male economy of desire and representation that defines woman in relation to himself. In this economy, women are either respectful mothers or witches, monsters, or prostitutes, etc. when they do not meet his demand of fulfilling the maternal role. Since both images are produced by the male desire, they are the two sides of the same coin.

In the light of this allusion to Genesis, who Laura and Iris are, becomes subject to the man who creates woman according to his desires. One of them is banished from the scene as the rival although they are actually defined in relation to the same position, the mother, in the male symbolic. As Laura communicates by recreating this picture like a code, Alex becomes the signifier allotting Laura and Iris their positions in this order. By the law of the phallus the sisters will be separated from each other.

Iris' marriage to Richard echoes the previous marriages in the Chase family. These marriages demonstrate the male subject's constitution of itself on the foundation of woman—mothers who are treated as commodities. The mothers in the family show significant similarities. The marriage of Adelia and Benjamin is the marriage of money and culture, in which Adelia as a mother-woman is expected to maintain Benjamin's self-representation as an upper-class man with her famous twelve-course dinners along with her decoration of the house that meet Benjamin's expectation of refinement and culture from her. Without Adelia, Benjamin has fortune but he also "want[s] Culture, or at least the concrete evidence of it. He want[s] the right china" (75). In this way, Adelia guarantees Benjamin's sense of being. Liliana, the next mother to enter the Chase family, marries money, too, but in her case, she brings religion instead of taste and culture since this is what Norval needs after having lost his mother. Norval finds the sense of union in Liliana's religious disposition which stems from again her losing her mother when she was nine. Thus, she and Norval share the longing for a union with the mother but since the union they seek is not with another person but with God as a substitute for the mother, they cannot achieve fulfillment in their marriage. Liliana's religious heritage will be owned by Laura, who like her mother, will prefer God and religion to money and worldly comforts that are substituted with the absence of the mother. Iris' marriage is different in that this time the Chase family exchange a woman with money because there is no son to continue the name of the father and they cannot take a woman to the family. With Iris, the male ancestry comes to an end in the Chase family. In the absence of a son, the family and together with the name of the father, the house, Avilion, ends up closed and in ruins as well.

Like Adelia, Iris is married to Richard to refine his coarse wealth with her relation to the aristocrat Adelia who is "married off" due to her poverty like Iris. Being offered to Richard like the amputated, mute virgins in the story of Sakiel-Norn, Iris commits herself to the role required of her without voicing her resentment and anger towards Richard even when her father dies in disillusionment upon Richard's closing down the factories. She behaves as a good girl using the strategy that she learned during their tutor Mr. Erskine's stay: "half-concealed insolence and silent resistance," which are common strategies for women who do not have the means and thus courage to resist openly the male pressure (203).

Iris' complicated feelings towards Laura and herself take a dangerous turn in her marriage with Richard. Although Laura makes it clear that she does not want to live with them, Iris turns a blind eye to her uneasiness in the house. Laura's attempts to share with Iris Richard's abuse are in vain; by reminding Iris of her disbelief of their tutor, Mr. Erskine's abuse when she was young, Laura implies that the scene of Mr. Erkine's abuse is repeated (481): Laura endures the abuse that takes place before Iris' eyes who does not believe what she sees, or Laura says. When Richard and Winifred imprison Laura in a clinic as Richard threatened to do so when she escaped on her way to Toronto, Iris collaborates with him and does not even visit Laura in the clinic (406). She knows very well that Laura does not lie, and she suspects whose fantasies she is trapped in— Richard's or her own (537). The word fantasy is significant here; Richard says that Laura thinks she is Iris because of her jealousy of Iris' status whereas it is Richard who fantasies that Laura and Iris are the same person and all women have the penis-envy that make them compete for the favor of men. Despite her suspicions, Iris does not do anything which means imprisoning Laura in the clinic with Richard and his sister, Winifred. As happens with Mr. Erskine's abuse, Reenie again figures as the woman who believes and helps Laura; she arranges the lawyer who is a cousin of the mothers which makes him trustworthy to get Laura out of the clinic. Submitting to the feminine role imposed on her, Iris herself becomes a tiger/wolf just like Winifred and Richard in her marriage as she herself realizes (403).

Iris' problematic relation to herself and other women is evident in her concern with her body and physical appearance. Feeling dirty after having sex with Richard, her anxiety about her body hair and frequent checks on her body shows Iris' perception of herself as the object of the male gaze, that is Richard's gaze that detects and humiliates her about her hair in the bathroom. In "Mechanics of Fluids" Irigaray argues that the bodily fluids like menstrual blood and mucus are the bodily remainders, *object a*, that contradict the logic of identity based on the solid ground of oneness of form (the phallus). Fluids (hair on the body can be counted among them) remind the male subject of the woman in the mother whom he rejects existence as the sexually different (*This Sex*, 108 -113). The male desire for the mother negates bodily fluids that belong to the other and Iris' distress shows that she is trapped in the male desire/gaze that objectifies her in the maternal function.

Similarly, the assumed vanity of women and their interest in their physical appearance is also related to the male subject's self-representation. Iris voices her deprivation of a way to express her anxiety when she mentions the interpretation of the image of woman looking into a mirror as the vanity of women whereas for Iris this image is the expression of the anxiety with her body (371). According to Freud, women's shame and sense of deficiency because they do not have a penis accounts for their vanity as a way of making up for this lack, however, Irigaray argues that the interest in clothing is a substitution for a language to articulate the desire of woman and the only way for women to raise their value in the market (*Speculum*, 114 -115). The attention Iris pays to clothing subtending her anxiety with her body is a sign of her imprisonment in the male desire. She envelopes herself in the expensive clothes, which is according to Irigaray the sign of women's lack of home, language to articulate their own desires in addition to the obligation to wrap themselves as commodities to maintain their value in the market (Whitford 1991, 143). Even at very odd moments like her father's funeral or visiting the morgue to identify her sister, her care for clothes shows to what extent Iris is in a deprivation of a language to express herself and her seeking comfort in clothes in her feeling of exile.

Upon running across Alex one day, Iris gets a chance to realize the romantic affair she was projecting on Adelia when she was a child despite her first-hand experience of marriage as an economic affair. Furthermore, she uses Alex to outdo Laura in her sub-conscious competition for the desire for the mother. While Richard is raping Laura and threatening to report Alex's place to the police, Iris meets with Alex in secret. Iris' final and fatal attack on Laura, which is telling her that she is informed of Alex's death in Europe as the next of kin because they were lovers, leads Laura to suicide. Iris manages to outdo Laura in the end, but it certainly does not bring satisfaction to her. As her marriage to Richard turns Iris into a mute virgin and a blind assassin, Laura's love for Alex turns her into the slave girl in an opera whose name is given to the scent Liu that Iris uses. As Iris implies Laura's fate is similar to that of this slave girl's "whose fate was to kill herself rather than betray the man she loved, who in his turn loved someone else" (295).

With Alex's stories, her affair with Alex offers Iris an opportunity to discover what is happening in her private life and her involvement in the political affairs. Through his stories, Alex communicates to Iris how their private sphere is entangled with the political sphere. Yet, since these stories are narrated by Iris in Alex's voice, it is possible to suspect that Iris herself wrote these stories using Alex as the narrator of them after she realized the circumstances of her marriage and life. In the story of Sakiel-Norn, the characters, the wars, and the plot are in parallel to the characters in the family, culture, and the exact time period in which the relationship takes place. Critics like Dancygier and Bouson point out the similarity between Iris and the amputated virgins that are sacrificed to the goddess. Dancygier also suggests that the king represents Norval as the symbol of the aristocracy whose doom has come with the rise of the middle-class and the lord of the underworld who initiates the plot against the king represents Richard as the symbol of the middle class (145). She concludes that it was Richard who hired Alex to burn the factory who is, like the blind assassins, is destroyed by the same class and becomes the same class' tool to assassinate others now.

Yet, there is more to the code in this story. While the lord of the underworld is contriving a plot against the king, which represents Richard's destruction of Norval, and the affair between the blind Alex and the mute Iris are on the crossroads of loving each other forever or Alex's murdering Iris, the people of joy, namely the Soviet troops under the command of Stalin, are marching into Europe to chop both the aristocrats and the new-middle class along with the proletariat for their "luxury" and "worship [of] the false gods" (145). Upon Alex's departure for the Spanish civil war against Franco, the story of Sakiel-Norn is left unfinished. Iris' suggestion for the end of the story is that Iris and Alex help the barbarians (the communists) invade the city and live happily with the utopic women community which is said to be settled at the outskirts of the city of Sakiel-Norn. This suggestion shows again Iris' naive belief that as individuals they are outside the destructive world. She selfishly wishes to escape even though this salvation will be other people's demise. The last episode that Alex writes before he is killed in the war disappoints Iris who is still in her dream world and expects the two of them can leave destruction behind, but the end Alex writes parallels the war affairs taking place. Now, the lizard men, who represent Hitler, break the ice between the capitalist and socialist to fight against the threat of total destruction. Yet, Alex's attempts to wake Iris are in vain; she is blind as well as mute.

The inner stories also reveal that the wars that seem to set the background of the history of the family reveal that both love and war are founded on the same logic, which is implied by the elderly Iris when she points out to how they follow each other: "And then, after the wedding, there was the war. Love, then marriage, then catastrophe" (87). War appears as the outcome of male desire to perpetuate his dominance in patriarchal culture. It is a way of sustaining the value invested in the phallus that always needs more property, earth, wealth, women, etc. Wars make the male violence explicit in its desire to own and accumulate for assuring and increasing his value whose logic is basically drawn on owning women. Therefore, it is not possible to understand political and economic structure as a separate domain from the *private* relationships—which means sexual relationships.

Although the parallel between the mute virgins and Iris is apparent, the theme of blindness is more prevalent and multi referential. It also implies how women serve men by competing with each other in their blindness which again results from their subjection to men, which Irigaray explains as:

> Without realizing it, or willing it, women constitute the most terrible instrument of their own oppression: they destroy anything that emerges from their undifferentiated condition and thus become agents of their own annihilation, their reduction to sameness that is not their own (*An Ethics* 88).

As the slave children who go blind by ceaseless weaving and are sold as prostitutes become pitiless assassins in the service of the class that torture them, women also become each other's assassins in the service of men that reduce them to commodities. Winifred's humiliation and domination of Iris, Laura's destruction by Iris who allies herself with Richard to destroy Laura are some of the examples that indicate how women participate in their own exploitation by men. By combining both the victimizer (assassin) and the victim (blind) in the title, "The Blind Assassin," Atwood indicates that there is no clear-cut distinction between these two roles. Victims, the blinded, can turn into victimizers and it is the wounds, the blindness that perpetuates the patriarchal culture. Rather than looking for the center of the patriarchal culture in the institutions and in the power holders, Atwood analyzes how the subjects become contributors to the culture through their incorporation into it. She points out to what makes a human being, and the complicated relationships among people that constitute patriarchal society together.

How women become each other's enemy in their desire for the mother that turns into rivalry is apparent in all the relations between the women in the novel; between Winifred and Iris, Reenie and Liliana, Iris and Myra. Winifred behaves like a mother to Iris when she is kissing her on the forehead, making decisions about her clothing, hobbies, house, and even her behaviors in society. As indicated by the misunderstanding of the nurse when Iris gave birth to Aimee, Richard and Winifred play parental roles in her life and this situation accounts for the faltering condition of Iris' marriage. Irigaray states that when woman is defined as the mother, men transfer their desire for the mother to their wives in future. Marriage serves the satisfaction of man's desire and this satisfaction secures the marriage, as articulated by Freud (*Speculum*, 42). What Richard seeks in his wife is his mother and the wife can have power as long as she satisfies his incestuous desire. Yet, instead of Iris, Winifred fulfills this function and thereby she becomes more powerful in Richard's life. Winifred's mothering Iris is combined with hatred since Iris is a threat to Winifred's position in Richard's life. Winifred can have power as long as she is the most important woman in Richard's life as his sister-mother. When Laura dies, Iris dissolves this relationship and after Richard's death, the tension and the silent rivalry between Iris and Winifred turn into an open hatred and war over Iris' daughter, Aimee who becomes no more than booty in the end. Winifred revenges herself by taking the custody of Aimee who destroys herself with alcohol and drugs in the end.

In addition to the problems that are created by taking the woman as the maternal function, the class barriers add to the problematic relationship between women. Alongside the mothers in the Chase family, there is another line of mothers in lower-class; Reenie's mother, Reenie and lastly Myra together with the upper-class women; Adelia, Liliana and Iris, all of whom occupy the place of the mother. Reenie's mother looks after Adelia, then Reenie takes up the role of mother for Iris and Laura when the mother is 'doing goods elsewhere' or is ill. After Reenie leaves, Myra takes over the job of looking after Iris. Nevertheless, these women are of a lower class, which adds further tension to their relationship with the middle-class women in the family. Reenie and Mrs. Hillcote, the servants, for example, share the feeling of envy/hatred of the middle-class. They gossip about Norval's artist friend Callista, who sculptures the war memorial "The Weary Soldier," about her clothing and behavior. Their comments express their antagonism against Callista's privileges as a middle-class woman.

Reenie criticizes Liliana for her devotion to religion and her helping the poor who according to Reenie do not deserve teaching. Reenie's comments on Liliana are dubious; she seems to be expressing her admiration of Liliana's goodness whereas the undertones give away her criticism that Liliana's teaching the poor is due to her inability to see the reality that the poor neither deserve teaching nor can learn according to Reenie (84). These comments, while on the surface appreciate Liliana's religiousness and goodness actually carry the tone of criticism of the mother; the mother does not behave as a proper middle-class woman. In *The Servant's Hand,* Robbins argues that servant figures in literature use various strategies to voice their reaction and discontent with their lower position in the family implicitly since they cannot speak up against the family. Irony is one of the forms that this discontent appears in Reenie's attitude. Reenie's relationship with the women in the family is thereby a complicated love and hate relationship in which rivalry in mothering and class antagonism are combined.

Yet, Reenie differs from the Murgatroyds, the servants whom Richard hires for their house in Toronto after Iris' father dies. Although they are of the same class as Reenie, their relation to the employer family stands on a different axis. This difference is recognized by Richard who sees Reenie as a threat to his domination and discards her from Avilion. Iris is also aware of this difference. She cannot differentiate the Murgatroyds members from each other and senses that they are a threat. Unlike the Murgatroyds, Reenie is not only a servant in the house. For Richard, Reenie is a threat to his power over the sisters because as Laura is well aware, she may back the sisters as she really does when Laura is imprisoned in a clinic.

This is because, Reenie stands in a different status as a servant— the servant whose relation to the family is not only a matter of exchange and does not stand on a monetary axis, but who is more like a member of the family. This relationship belongs to the society before the rise of the middle-class in the nineteenth century in which the concept of the family includes the servants as well and this status leads to both love and hatred for the family (Horn 1975, 109). While they live in the same house and work for the family, they have a lower status. Reenie's status at home is close to that of the children, the sisters; the underprivileged members and this brings the children and the servants closer but still, the fact that the servant will remain where she is whereas the children will grow up to be masters and mistresses creates tension between them. Thus, the relationship between Reenie and the sisters has two dimensions intertwined: the substitute mother and substitute daughters—confusion of identity, and the servant and mistresses—class barriers in the way of love.

This problematic is erased in the relations in the house of the new money by erasing the old family structure: the Murgatroyds' relation to the family is based on a monetary basis: there is no personal relationship between the servant and the master/mistress. Richard pays them, he is the boss, so they are loyal to him. As to Reenie and the father, there are ambiguities according to Iris. Iris suspects that Reenie's daughter, Myra could have been fathered by her father, Norval (476). Taking the blurring of the difference between women into consideration, this can be true; the substitute-mother could also have become the substitute-wife for Norval after his wife dies. If this is so, Reenie's criticism of the mother and Callista can also be interpreted as jealousy. In addition, the elderly narrator's casting doubt on the fatherhood (of Myra's father) is also part of her aim to subvert the patriarchal culture by emphasizing the maternal heritage.

The problematic relationship between Reenie and Iris is also marked by the similarities between them. Iris shares the responsibility of taking care of Laura with Reenie and thus becomes a rival to Reenie in motherhood, but she fails. After Laura's escape from the clinic with Reenie's help, Iris feels guilty for her failure in looking after Laura but at the sa'e time, she still wants to prove herself to Reenie as a mother by showing Aimee's picture to show that at least she managed to have a baby if not become a good mother to her sister. Reenie, on the other hand, discards Iris because first she herself became a mother so she cannot mother Iris anymore and then she sees that Iris cannot be trusted as a mother. Being both a substitute mother and a rival, Reenie is both someone to outdo and to be asked for approval. In Reenie, Iris sees what she is supposed to be, a mother, and her failure in doing so. Yet, Reenie has her own failures in complying with the requirements of society from the mother-woman; despite her preaching moral values for appropriate female behavior, she gets pregnant before she gets married. Therefore, Reenie's distance from Iris has the traces of her sense of guilt due to her failure to be the appropriate model-mother as she instructed the sisters when they were children.

Although Iris is aware of her complicity in the destruction of Laura which led to the destruction of Aimee as well while she is writing down the history of the family, it is not possible to say that her relationship with Myra does not still stand on the axis of mothering. Myra now has the function of a mother: she is the one who looks after Iris and takes care of her physical being; her eating, seeing the doctor, maintaining the house, etc. Iris, in return, in the place of the daughter, shows a silent resistance that is combined with love and hatred and moreover, she allies herself with Myra's husband, Walter, against Myra. Like a child resisting against an overprotective mother, she resists Myra in curious ways; her attempt to do the laundry by herself, or her rejection to see a doctor for instance (448). Here, Atwood again stresses that to become a woman is not only a matter of war in a marriage with the male power but also a matter of learning to create relationships in which women can recognize each other as individuals. The relationships among women based on mothering prevent them from loving each other which means from loving themselves as well, since all women play the role of the mother and these relationships result in tension which blurs the distinction between love and hatred.

Iris' failure to comply with the requirements of being a mother ends Richard's name, too. As she herself is aware, Iris cannot become a good mother to Aimee, which can be explained with her mother's death that *"change[s] everything"* as she states (107, italics in the original). The mother's real absence, and then separation from Reenie, the mother-substitution, leaves the sisters without a mother figure to reflect themselves on to become a mother-woman. Iris gets struck in the place of the mother whose death she takes as a treachery and whose place is void now. She is aware that she does not have the capacity to love so she names her baby Aimee, the loved.

However, Aimee cannot love and be loved either without a mother to reflect herself on. When Laura dies, Iris, this time, consciously rejects her role. To   ulfil her role as a mother, Iris should have ignored Richard's rape of Laura and continued her marriage, but she chooses to leave and moreover take revenge on Richard. By rejecting her role as a good mother, she also leaves Aimee without a mother figure to model herself on. Aimee, who cannot see a way to love and to be loved, destroys herself in return. Brought up with the silent hatred of her mother against

Richard first and then with Winifred's for her mother, she destroys herself
to destroy the hateful mothers, Winifred and Iris. Aimee's failure or
rejection to *become a mother* manifests itself in her not nourishing her
daughter Sabrina, too. When a woman, here Aimee, does not become *a
mother*, she is left as a residue of society; a marginal, an outsider. The real
lack of a mother, or a proper mother figure—as in the case of Aimee—
leads to the destruction of the women in the family. Since men need
woman-mothers to transfer their name and property to their sons, women's
rejection of the role of the mother means the destruction of the fathers.
Iris' divorce ends Richard's name like Norval's, who lost his wife and did
not have a son either to continue his name.

The gynaecological illnesses that almost all mothers in the Chase
family suffer from indicate women's painful imprisonment in the maternal
function. Adelia and Liliana die of illnesses due to childbearing and lack
of health care related to birth control. Laura can also be thought of as a
woman who suffers from gynaecological causes in the sense that her
imprisonment in the clinic and suicide eventually are related to her getting
pregnant by Richard. These gynaecological problems imply that women's
reproductive function, and the imposing of the role of the mother on
women result in disastrous ends including death.

Men's dependence on woman-mothers who nourish but never
drink too much, have sex out of marriage like Bertha Mason in *Jane Eyre*
or who does not seek a divorce because of a rape as Iris does is the
condition of the perpetuation of the family. Iris' failure and rejection of the
maternal role explains why both the Chase and Griffen families have
vanished. The fate of houses parallels the fate of the name of the fathers.
When Norval dies, Avilion is closed and in the end, it is in ruins. The bad
condition of Iris' house indicates the absence of the law, name of the
father since houses are owned by man and kept by mother-women.

Besides the fact that Iris is not attached to a man and even does
not live in her family home, Avilion, which has become a curiosity of the
town, her writing makes her homeless in patriarchal society; her home is
now language. Myra and her husband Walter's endeavor to repair the
house shows their wish to sustain the family institution and Iris' struggle
against patriarchy manifests itself in her not heeding the well-being of her
house. Bouson mentions that Atwood describes *BA* as "Jane Austen in a

very black mode" (qtd. in Bouson 2003, 257). *BA* resembles *Pride and Prejudice* in that, in both novels, houses appear as the symbol of the family institution based on the father-son relationships (Austen 1994). Patriarchy is founded on men's dependence on women to sustain their houses, names, and thereby identity.

The representation of woman as mother who exists as the satisfier of needs and nourishing also turns the mother into both mysterious, frightening slaves, and enemies. Iris writes:

> (What fabrications they are, mothers. Scarecrows, wax dolls for us to stick pins into, crude diagrams. We deny them an existence of their own, we make them up to suit ourselves- our own hungers, our own wishes, our own deficiencies. Now that I've been one myself, I know) (116).

The non-representation of woman and the rejection of sexual difference leads to sense of guilt and a fear of women in society. Irigaray says that this lack of acknowledgement of the mother as a woman that she calls matricide is silenced in culture and replaced by the concept of patricide as the constituting element of culture. This matricide, though silenced, shows itself as fear and violence against women as a form of defense. On social level, "the resistances and defences which conceal the original crime of matricide" show itself in the frightening stories of dead women as appear in the inner story, for instance, in which "the victim comes back to haunt the slayer in the form of persecutory anxiety" (Whitford 1991, 34). The stories of dead women who live in caves and devour passer-bys that are narrated in the inner story imply a fear of revenge; aggression, which results in paranoia and fear, is the acknowledgement of the crime. Women appear as the castrating mothers who threaten man's sense of being which is built on his investment in the value of the phallus by representing the other sex, the vagina as "a nothing see" that threatens his logic of identity based on the oneness of the form of the phallus (*Speculum*, 47). Woman's vagina and her lack of the phallus represents castration, the recognition of which horrifies men.

In the story of Sakiel-Norn told by Alex, women's making human beings in clay and in bread for children for the rebirth ritual of the king furthers the idea that the male subjectivity, its unity is based on the relation to the maternal function of women. The Goddess' giving life to the god/king by gathering the fragmented body of him is represented by the women's making an image of the god/king in clay and in bread for children. Here, women's reproductive function serves the unity of the male subject whereas this function and woman is not represented in culture. In this representation, women are disempowered by being turned into a supporter of the male since it is the king/god who holds the power in society. Representing women's making bread instead of giving birth, now, is the result of women's losing their status in society as the guardians of fertility. Now they are loaf-givers; providing the male with the food/blood to attain his wholeness. In this context, Reenie's making bread in the shape of human being for Iris and Laura, and Liliana's death on a bread day become significant. They indicate the irony of women's status and the representation of reproduction; while women are trapped in their maternal function, this function is not represented in the formation of subjectivity. Irigaray says that this lack of representation of the desire of/for the mother is the fundamental sacrifice that ensures man's identity and culture. Then, the mother's death on the bread day is not different from the sacrifice of the virgins who are silenced by the amputation of their tongues in the story of Sakiel-Norn. Irigaray explains that

> Patriarchy is founded upon the theft and violation of the daughter's virginity and the use of her virginity for commerce between men, including religious commerce [...]. Patriarchy has constructed its heaven and hell upon this original sin. It has imposed silence upon the daughter. It has dissociated her body from her speech, and her pleasure from her language. It has dragged her down into the world of male drives, a world where she has become invisible and blind to herself, her mother, other women and even men, who perhaps want her that way (*Thinking*, 112).

In the story of Sakiel-Norn, the world of male drives is represented by the Lord of the Underworld who rapes the virgin girls before their sacrifice. It is noteworthy that this lord refers to Hades, the god of the underworld, who separates Demeter from her daughter Persephone. It is believed that if the girls do not go through this torture and sacrifice, they will be punished by interdiction, that is, they will be one of those dead women with azure hair from whom Iris gets the strength to continue writing (142). This land of dead women is the hell that is created by the male desire; the world of the female silenced desire that appears in the male's nightmares as the castrating women like Medusa.

Women's closeness to the productive, fertile nature that was symbolized and guarded by the mother-daughter couple is distorted into the form of cooking for the family. The association of women and cookery is mentioned in the epigraph by John Ruskin in Adelia's cookbook. Here, Ruskin mentions women from mythology as model women, but as a child Iris realizes the problem in Ruskin's images of women as loaf-givers: the women he mentions are impossible to imagine "rushing around in the kitchen" like Reenie (221). Medea who kills her children to take revenge from her husband is a witch who can make magic potions and clothes, and a fortune teller. Circe, the Greek goddess, again a master of herbs and plants turns men into pigs. In *The Odyssey*, she invites the men to a feast where she offers magic potions to turn them into pigs from which Odysseus protects himself with a magic herb called moly that can only come from celestial hands, in this case from Hermes. Helen of Troy, the daughter of Leda and Zeus, causes war among men and also her beauty/body has such an attractive power that Menelaus drops his sword at the sight of her body and cannot take revenge. The Queen of Sheba though has no connection with magic, is a very wealthy and powerful queen. These mythological women, although turned into model images in Ruskin's depiction as the model mother figure whose function in society is reduced to cooking for the family, disclose a different order. The combination of cookery and witchcraft together in these mythological characters also indicates that what is thought as witchcraft is no more than women's wisdom of plants and herbs. Women's knowledge of nature which is also the ground of modern medicine is now represented as witchcraft, which is what Carter elaborates on with the witchlike character, Liz, in *NC*.

Today, what is left of this connection between women and nature in patriarchal culture is the role of the nourishing mothers, the "loaf-givers" (221). Cooking is now part of women's domestic role in the house that belongs to a patriarch. Reenie's cooking is a maternal function; nourishing both physically and mentally; she gives food-candies to sooth the girls when they are crying. As a substitute mother, she represents the nourishing body that the male culture is still attached to. The knowledge of plants and herbs that is of nature is incorporated into the patriarchal culture by turning it into cooking as part of the maternal role. However, women's connection to nature stood on a different axis before the establishment of patriarchal culture: on the mother-daughter relationships that Irigaray explains as follows:

> At one time mother and daughter formed a natural and social model. The mother-daughter couple was the guardian of the fertility of nature in general, and of the relationship with the divine. In that era, food consisted of the fruits of the earth. The mother-daughter couple safe-guarded human food and the site of oracular speech [...] (*Thinking*, 12).

The violation of this couple by the male desire that is represented by Hades or Richard and Alex in *BA* transforms the connection of women to nature into irrationality and thereby condemns fertility. Women as the guardians of fertility are diminished to cooking for the family that is founded on the male ancestry or the name of the fathers. The violation of the maternal ancestry constitutes a destructive world that condemns fertility and men always want more of everything; women, children, earth, money, without ever feeling fulfilled.

The importance of religion in placing the connection between women and nature as a residue in the symbolic system is implied in *The Odyssey*: women are defeated with the help of the celestial hands—Hermes, the god. In order to defy Circe's magical food that men cannot fight against, the god, Hermes, provides Odysseus with an herb against Circe's influence. Here, there is the idea that women's knowledge of nature, cooking can challenge men's power but the idea of god can help men supersede women's power. That the idea of difference is not recognized, women, women's closeness to nature, or their sexual organs become a threat to the male identity. To maintain his unity, oneness, God helps men to overcome their fear of the "nothing to see," so this is a war between men and women; the gods and the goddess. Women's witchcraft, religion, representation, and subjectivity is defied by the male religion; the idea of God disempowers women by turning them into the mother of man/god, and thereby erases their position as active agents in society. In other words, their magic potions (food and closeness to nature), their knowledge, and contribution to society are turned into supernatural, witchcraft as a negative term; irrational which is defined by the male rational. That is to say, women as belonging to the realm of the irrational operate as the other of man who represents the rational. The mythology underlying the patriarchal society excludes the representation of woman other than the mother of man and represents woman as the other of man. In this way, women's knowledge is excluded from the male realm of knowledge by representing it as irrationality and superstition. Irigaray says that religion functions as a regulator in the relationships between men; the relationship between god and man or the father and the son by providing the unique being on which the male subject reflects himself, which ensures the idea of sexual sameness: "For lack of thinking this ground [sexual difference], the relation to God is imposed on us as fundamental cause of unity (and) of thinking—for the world and for man" (*The Way* 72). The relationship between Hermes and Odysseus, as the father-son, man-god, then is the emblem of the patriarchal society; it represents the establishment of a whole system based on the exchange among men, which is as Irigaray says, a hom(m)osexual market in which the alliance between God and man repudiate the representation of woman as a subject (*This Sex*, 171).

Related to cooking, eating also has implications about the formation of subjectivity. The difference in Laura's and Iris' eating habits is connected with their different relation to their identity as women. As a child, Iris is fond of eating; she, for example, eats both pieces of the cake Reenie makes for their birthday after the mother's death whereas Laura refuses to eat hers when she hears that eating might hurt her mother (173). For Laura, eating is a betrayal of her mother, a sort of cannibalism. She also refuses to eat the rabbit because it is similar to the baby that her mother miscarried. In addition, she collects the man-shaped breads that Reenie makes and when they are found in her drawers, she wants a funeral for them. If eating is cannibalism, feeding on the mother's blood she will not eat or become a mother. Iris, however, is a cannibal "gnawing" at the bones by eating a lot and now by writing though now she eats very little (43); her realization of her own collaboration in Laura's destruction, her sense of guilt results in a change in her towards her body and what she takes into her body. And these indicate a change in her sense of identity. Now, her cannibalism is her writing; she writes with her sister's blood which is also her own; the blood of woman.

The mythological figures that appear throughout the novel imply a war between woman and man or between the maternal and paternal line. Iseult and Tristan, the nymphs at the pond, Dido, Europa, Danae, and Leda (the queen of Sheba, Helen of Troy, Circe, and Medea are discussed in the context of cookery) function as the models for the image of woman in Western culture. They are fictitious women proposed as model for women, or they represent the triumph of the male ancestry over the maternal ancestry. The Irish princess Iseult, for instance, is depicted as the ideal romantic lover, whereas her affair with Tristan is actually an adulterous affair with Tristan and there is the effect of love potion-magic. The reality of her life is erased to represent her as the ideal woman. Leda is raped by Zeus in the disguise of a swan but in art, Leda and the swan are depicted as they make love. The image of Europa kidnapped by Zeus in the shape of a bull functions as a threat of men's power over women. It is noteworthy that Mr. Erskine indulges in making the sisters read this story. Similarly, Danae's imprisonment by her father, Acrisius whose name is in danger without a son, to prevent her from giving birth to a son is a fight between the maternal and paternal ancestry. The oracle tells Acrisius that he will be killed by his daughter's son and upon this, he imprisons Danae. Acrisius' aim is to prevent the maternal line, his daughter's child from replacing the paternal line, which is already in danger. These mythological events show a struggle between men and women or as Irigaray says between the maternal and paternal genealogies and they show how patriarchy is established, "the negative moment" by the defeat of women (Whitford 1991, 102 -103). The tension and war between the maternal and paternal line, or man and woman, accompanies the tension in the plot between men and women. These mythological figures and the events that they refer to shed further light on the cause of the problems between men and women in *BA*.

The story of the two sisters presents the patriarchal culture that effaces peace and love among women and men for the perpetuation of patriarchal culture that depends on the father-son relationship and on women's reduction to the status of a commodity. This culture is jeopardized when women do not carry out their maternal role as the guardian of men's home or as the carrier of their heirs. Aimee's daughter Sabrina leaves the reader with the possibility of change in the social order for her position in the paternal line is a mystery. Aimee's father is not Richard but Alex. By choosing this name, Atwood alludes to Daniel Defoe's *Roxanna* in which Roxanna's daughter, Amy is deprived of her maternal heritage. Unlike Defoe who places suspicion on the identity of the mother, Atwood destabilizes the paternal heritage. Thus, Sabrina's paternal ancestry is unknown like Alex', who was found in the ruins of houses alone as a baby in the World War 1. Her father is unknown even to her mother, Aimee. On the other hand, Sabrina's heritage on the maternal line is reliable. By defining Sabrina's identity and heritage on the maternal line, Atwood suggests a reconstruction of identity that recognizes the desire of/for the mother. In addition, the meta-narration by Iris indicates the way out of this vicious circle of hatred, which is through the very constitutive element of it at the same time, namely, language, to which I will turn now.

2.2. The Deadly Interplay of Reality and Fiction

The story of the two sisters that demonstrates the devastative consequences of the lack of female subjective identity in patriarchal culture is framed by the narrator's comments on the time and the act of writing. The frame narration puts fiction on a crucial status in the formation of identity and indicates how dangerous fiction can become when individuals get trapped in it. In addition to Iris' comments on writing, the intricate structure of *BA,* renders the narration, like *NC,* a meta-narration that discusses the relation between art and life, the nature of fiction, and the nature of language. The narrator, Iris now in her old age shares with the reader the obstacles for her to narrate her past, which amounts to exposing the fictionality of the novel itself. The narrator is very much concerned and anxious about fiction and writing since it has so much power that it can even replace what is real and become deadly. Atwood elaborates on "[t]he tyranny of Art" over the formation of identity and also how art, that is, writing, can help woman to create herself a new subjectivity like Angela Carter (176).

Iris' failure to realize what is happening before her eyes results from her creating her identity in fiction, male fantasy that she submits to. Like Pip in *Great Expectations* who founds his identity on the inscriptions on his parents' grave when he is a child, Iris builds her sense of identity upon fiction. What she hears from Reenie, who is probably no more than seven or eight years older than her, about her grandparents and parents forms her idea of herself. Yet, Reenie is not a dependable source:

> What she would tell me varied in relation to my age, and also in relation to how distracted she was at the time. Nevertheless, in this way I collected enough fragments of the past to make a reconstruction of it, which must have born as much relation to the real thing as a mosaic portrait would to the original (83).

Depending on Reenie's accounts, which is not very consistent, Iris creates a past and an identity for herself. Thus, Adelia and Liliana's courage under physical sufferings, Adelia and Benjamin's aristocratic marriage, the romantic courtship of Norval, and Norval's courage in war form the shaky fictive ground on which she will gain her sense of identity and of the outer world as well. This imaginary ground will shape her life in future, especially her marriage and her affair with Alex. For instance, she will take her love affair with Alex as her childhood fiction of Adelia's meeting a secret lover in the garden come true. Neither what Laura says, nor the clues that Alex gives in the story of the Sakiel-Norn are enough to wake her up from her dream world. It is only with Laura's death that she faces the real world. Her suicide shatters the life that Iris thought they had been living and her identity that she had reflected on Laura, and then she realizes what Winifred and Richard with her own cooperation had done to Laura. Having learned the extent to which fiction can subvert reality, she turns to fiction to take her revenge from Richard who is trapped in the fantasy of woman, the fantasy that Laura and Iris are the same person and that his sexual abuse can satisfy them. In return of the male fantasy of woman and love that imprisoned and destroyed her and Laura's life, she reciprocates with her own fiction, titled "The Blind Assassin" that first ends Richard's political career and then kills him.

Iris' fiction, "The Blind Assassin," also leads to a ceaseless war between Winifred and Iris after Richard's death. Winifred reciprocates Iris' revenge with this book by taking Aimee from Iris. The circumstances and consequences of the book's publication demonstrate the extent to which art and life are intertwined so as to make it impossible to see them as separate domains. Whether the writer of this story is Laura or Iris in reality actually does not matter since the truth that the story gives is the truth of a woman's experience; whether the sister-in-law or the wife, women are trapped in the marriage institution and abused by the patriarch who assumes that they can be happy in this situation.

Newspaper articles about the events of the family point out to how reality can be subverted in writing, even in the one that claims to give facts instead of fiction. This difference between writing and reality is introduced first by the newspaper article about the death of Laura that puts the suicide as an accident to protect Richard's reputation (6). Similarly, the article about Iris' marriage gives the official version of marriage institution. Marriage is an event to be celebrated, an event that is thought to give happiness to the couple whereas in reality it is an exchange among men to keep their status. The articles present the reader with the accounts of life in harmony with the dominant values of society. In other words, the news gives the "official" account of events; the society must live in the illusion of the happy marriage so that this institution can continue to be the economic and ideological ground of society.

The use of photography plays an important role in the discussion of art's effects on life. The third section of the novel is on the picture of Alex with Iris on the corner of which Laura's hand is visible. In the picture, Alex is holding up his hand "to protect himself from the camera, from the person who must be there, taking the picture; or else to protect himself from those in the future who might be looking in at him through this square, lighted window of glazed window" (8). What Alex is protecting himself from is art, here photography, and also writing that refers to the novel itself. The "square, lighted window of glazed paper" of the photograph is aggressive because of its power to impose the artist's view of reality which can contradict the experience of the subject that turns out to be the art-object in the photograph.

The photographer Murray's taking a picture of Laura and Iris with Alex on the factory picnic places suspicion on Alex since he appears as the seducer of the factory owner's daughters and this picture can be used as evidence for accusing him of burning the factory. Alex's holding his hand is an attempt to prevent the photographer from imposing an identity on him as the enemy of the upper-middle class or a socialist. In addition to referring to the photographer who creates an identity for him, Alex's self-protective gesture can also be interpreted as an objection to the reader (us) who is now like the person looking at the picture will give him an identity again. The photograph or writing about him, art portrays a different Alex than the one he creates for himself; both the artist and the reader/viewer create an Alex. In Murray's photograph, he is a suspect, in Laura's, he is the male subject as the signifier that prevents the two sisters from coming together. In the inner story "The Blind Assassin" he is a socialist in a love affair with an upper-middle class woman telling stories about the underlying ideology of patriarchal society that affronts her for her marriage. In *BA*, he is the blind assassin in love with the mute Iris who tells stories of the circumstances of their relationship and ponders to find a way out of the pattern that they are placed in their relationship through these stories. Each arrangement of the picture and the characters in the hands of a different writer, photographer or reader, viewer imputes a different significance to the same object.

The discussions over the war memorial, "The Weary Soldier," reveal art's function in and power over society by emphasizing that representation is an ideological matter. What is at stake in art is not what is real but it is what the artist, the public, or the institution that produces or orders the art believe the real to be. In other words, art is the product of the culture which represents the culture's values and ideology. As a war memorial, the public wants a heroic, victorious soldier whereas in reality the soldiers are shattered physically and mentally. The father with one eye, a leg, and the belief in God, in the purpose of the war—the good of the world—lost, can no longer believe in the triumphant image of the soldier who willingly self-sacrificed (180). The image of heroic soldier and the belief in waging war for the good of society is a fiction created for the public whereas a soldier is a scattered body and mind, and war is destruction. The shape that art gives to reality is thus not an innocent one; it functions as an ideological tool to offer the masses the way they should perceive and accept reality. If the public saw the shattered soldiers as memorials, the wars could not be welcomed that easily and the triumphs could no longer be received cheerfully.

When fiction is such a powerful tool to govern masses and create identities, it is only natural that Iris now is so concerned with her writing and questions the nature of language and fiction. As soon as Iris starts writing about her past, the reason for writing that includes the question of the identity of the reader and the writer as well emerges as the main issue for her. These ponderings on writing shows a progress. That is to say, Iris thinks through writing not only her reasons but also the nature of language which ends up as the locus of her identity.

Iris takes up the pen when she learns that she has a heart disease, that death is not far (52). From then on, she starts reflecting on her purpose in writing about her and Laura's life while she is writing her past. The old, isolated narrator in her collapsing house, like her body, starts with various reasons. First, she feels that she needs some kind of proof of her existence, since death announces its arrival soon in addition to her being almost erased from society/life all alone in a house. Writing, then, is "a claim to existence" (603). In *Negotiating with the Dead*, Atwood says that writing is also striving against death, mortality by leaving something that will continue to assert one's existence after the body perishes. In Iris' case, leaving her autobiography and Laura's biography behind can be a way of dealing with the threat of oblivion in the form of death. Writing is also a desire to "to leave a proof, a message" to someone; that is, to convey to somebody what she knows and has experienced (513). Apart from claiming her own existence and truth, Iris also wants "to get the blood off [her] hands" to excuse herself in a guilty conscience for destroying Laura's life (603). Although sense of guilt is one of the most important driving motives, this writing is more than confession. It is also a defense; an explanation of how Iris or a woman becomes a "wolf", "given the proper circumstances" (403). In this sense, the narrator suggests that this destructiveness is not due to the natural wolf-ness in a person but it is created in a given social structure which can make anyone a wolf.

However, her reason for writing becomes clear in the end through reflecting on her addressee; the "you" that the "I" in writing necessarily assumes in the syntax of language. The inscriptions in the washrooms, on banks, trees, or books, memorials, all writing, art are a message for someone and left as a proof of existence that is possible with a reader without whom there would be unendurable silence, absence or, in other words, there would be no language. Writing is impossible without a reader whether this reader is a known person or a hypothetical one; the "you," or the reader that emerges with the "I" of Iris in the syntax. Thereby, the identity and motive of the reader necessarily enter the discussion on the motive for writing. The "you" for Iris takes up various identities; it is at first "a witness," then, she addresses Myra and eventually the reader becomes Sabrina but the reader is also Iris herself (118). Iris broods on her motive for reading Laura's notebooks in such a way that the reader feels an urge to question her own reading of *BA* because the first person narration creates a sense of identification with the writer and also because the narrator is writing about her reading. What drives Iris to read Laura's notebooks is a combination of different needs and feelings: love, hatred, craving for knowledge, to learn who Laura is, what happened and also curiosity that is a sort of voyeurism, the satisfaction in watching, reading about other people (603). Reading and grave robbing resemble each other in the sense that in both actions the desire to learn about a person or to get something (such as knowledge or power) from the dead is the driving motive. Bringing herself and the reader together in the desire for reading, she makes the reader identify with Iris, the narrator, that is "the tiger" (403).

The necessity of the reader, the "you" in writing, even if this "you" is the "I" of the now writing subject—that is, the "I" that is writing now can become the reader, the "you" when reading the writing at a later time—has effects on what is written in return; writing the truth is impossible: "The only way you can write the truth is to assume that what you set down will never be read. Not by any other person, and not even by yourself at some later date. Otherwise you begin excusing yourself" (345). Then, since writing always addresses a reader who can even be yourself reading what you wrote before, writing the truth or writing without a reader is impossible. The truth of writing, the subject in writing becomes subject to the structure of language. That is to say that, language is a structure that structures life, the consciousness of the individual; what can be written and how it can be written.

Iris and her experience are subject to language, which makes the reality in writing the reality of language. The truth of the written word is impossible because there is also the absence, what is not written: "I look back over what I've written and I know it's wrong, not because of what I've set down, but because of what I've omitted. What isn't there has a presence, like the absence of light" (345). Derrida says that meaning of the written word is constructed through both the presence of the words and what is not written, the absence. The presence cannot be thought of without the absence that it excludes and so the absence is also, what makes the presence. Derrida calls these interdependent couples on which western thought is based violent hierarchies that make the meaning unstable.

Although the Western thought claims to give the truth through these oppositions, Derrida states that since meaning is constructed in a system of differences, through infinite substitutions meaning can never be stable, consistent. Therefore, it is not possible to get a consistent, unique meaning. Absence becomes absence with the presence, light becomes light with the dark, etc. Each arrangement of the absences and presences will create a different meaning. In *BA*, what the narrator calls wrong is then inherent in language; the attempt to convey the truth is doomed to fail for the truth of language is based on the determination of presence, an absolute truth which is actually absent. Whatever she writes will gain meaning together with what she does not write. The trouble for the woman writer is that as a woman she occupies the absence part in this construction of meaning.

Writing will never give the truth or life; it has its own sphere with its own rules of inclusion and exclusion. Writing cannot write the "voice outside the window" or "the wind"; "the living bird is not its labeled bones" (484). Iris' narration then turns out to be her struggle with the limits of language. The syntax of language necessitates the position of both the "I" and the "you," which produces the meaning in language. Without writing, that is without the novel, *BA*, there is no Iris; she is what is created in the writing; thereby "I [is] everybody's letter" (110). The subject in writing emerges as an effect of language but these positions are artificial ones that can be filled by anybody; "you" can become "I," "I" can become "you":

> [...]
> but Thou is a slippery character. Every Thou I've known has had a way of going missing. They skip town or turn perfidious, or else they drop like flies, and then where are you?
> Right about here (55).

With these comments and plays on the structure of language, Atwood points out to the construction of the subject in language, or the construction of Iris in writing. The subject, the narrator is created in the process of writing that imposes its own rules by creating the slippery positions of "I" and "you." To reinforce the idea of construction of the subject in writing, Iris also discloses the unreliability of her description of her parents and grandparents, when for example she is describing her mother: "(what was she wearing? Reenie knew this too [...])", or her grandfather: "Or, this is what is said of him in *The Chase Industries: A History,* a book my grandfather commissioned in 1903 and had privately printed [...]" (86; 68). The allusion to Anthony Burgess' *A Clockwork Orange* by using the same name, Alex, for the narrator of the science-fiction stories and the reference to the opening sentence of *A Clockwork Orange* in the opening of "The Blind Assassin," "What is it going to be then eh" and "What will it be then?" again direct the reader to language as the producer of the subject (Burgess 2000, 3; 11). Burgess, too suggests the creation of the subject in language through the inventive use of language that produces an effect of alienation of language on the reader and the creation of the narrator, Alex, through writing.

Eventually, as the narration nears the end, Iris determines who the "you" is. She discards Myra because she does not trust her much and suspects that she might burn the contents of her "trousseau," and then Sabrina, her granddaughter, on whom she depends for taking care of her writings (291). When burning the manuscripts or publishing them is accepted as metaphor for reading the novel, Myra is the woman who will not listen to/read Iris and think that it is best to keep the secrets in the family and Sabrina is the woman who will read and publish the manuscripts. Then we, the readers, become Sabrina. When the narrator reaches a decision about the identity of her reader, the "you," her reason for writing becomes clear in the closing sentences of the novel: "You are free to reinvent yourself at will" (627); "But I leave myself in your hands. What choice do I have? By the time you read this last page, that-if anywhere- is the only place I will be" (637). The subject is constructed in language and writing is the desire for an identity. The concern with reasons for writing, the limits of language inherent in its syntax and the logic of discourse, difficulty writing about life in total accumulate to the problematic position of the woman writer in language.

Iris, or the woman writer that is "[a] tabula rasa, not waiting to write, but to be written on" like the art object, Laura, struggles to accede to a subject position while being allocated in the logic of language to silence, to the position of lack, or the other as a woman (57). This is the strain of the *commodity who decides to go to the market on her own* but since this market (language) is dominated by men, she has to bend, play, struggle with the rules (*This Sex*, 196). The intertextuality and the meta-narration accomplish this end by exposing the rules of this representation. In order to speak as a woman, the subject has to turn the pen, the gaze on itself, on the subject who is speaking in the position of this slippery "I," which Atwood does as a woman writer writing about a woman (Iris) writing about a woman (Laura).

When it is considered that subjectivity is constructed in language that delegates the female to silence in order to make the male speech, meaning possible, language becomes the locus of the woman writer's quest for subjectivity. The logic of discourse based on the oppositions like the absence and presence brings forth a criticism of language since, in this construction of meaning, woman occupies the place of lack or the other. Fiction and language figure as the main issue for both woman and the writer whose uneasiness is doubled by being a woman writer. The variety of narrative techniques in *BA* subverts the subject-object dichotomy by directing the reader to focus on the act of writing and reading, and by putting the reader in a more active position. The complicated narrative technique with three narrators—the first-person narration by Iris in the frame story, the third person in the inner story "The Blind Assassin," and Alex as the narrator of the stories in the inner story—propounds the concept of fiction and art as the main theme in the novel.

Apart from the effect of the first-person narration and the discussion on the desire for reading, the story telling in the inner story also impels the reader to identify with Iris. The reader finds herself in the position of the listener of Alex's stories and in this way Atwood achieves a fascinating effect by shifting the position of the writer and the reader and introduces the reader into *BA*. Alex becomes Atwood when he says "thick plots are my specialty. If you want a thinner kind, look elsewhere." When we consider the thick plot of *BA* we become Iris and say "[a]ll right. Go on" with Iris to Atwood/Alex (147).

BA shares with *NC* the challenge to literary tradition through the allusion to oral tradition. Alex's story telling alludes to oral tradition in that it is more like a performance before the audience who interrupts, provides comments, and reacts to the story. This is a collaborative production as it is evident in the pronoun "we" that Iris uses: "We didn't say anything about children" (26). Alex takes into consideration Iris' suggestions and Iris objects when she feels offended by the implications like Alex's comparison of the sacrificial virgins to "a pampered society bride," that is herself (37). In addition to the performance of tale telling in the inner story, the frame narrator's expressions like "I take up the burden of my tale," "I pay out my line" also refer to oral tradition (167).

In *Negotiating with the Dead*, Atwood discusses the differences between the tale teller and the writer that came about with the age of printing (Atwood 2002). The main difference between these two forms is that in writing the time of creating and receiving is separated from each other and this separation between the listener and teller lead to a sense of duality in the writer's view of himself/herself as well. The writer's image in the book and the fame it invokes cast a shadow on and moreover belittle the individual who wrote the book. As the magnificence of the book contradicts the ordinary, banal existence of the body of the individual writer, the idea of double character of the writer emerges as a need especially for the romantic poet since the romantic poet finds himself in a dubious position in performing the necessary activities in the daily life while he claims himself to be a genius and his art to be the expression of this genius self. The duality in the character of the writer helps to preserve the god-like position of the writer relegating the banal condition of the body to somebody else (to the individual).

Also, in *The Author*, Bennett discusses oral tradition in comparison to the print age and illustrates the difference with the polemics on the identity of Homer. He points out to the problem of applying the modern concept of the writer on the concept of art and artist before the print age. He states that the attempt to find about the identity of Homer as the author of works that are attributed to him is in vain, because Homer's art was telling the stories that were told by many other poets with the addition of his own contribution and interpretation. The writer writing by himself is the image of the romantic artist that emerged with the print age.

Therefore, Homer is a name that covers all of the poets of this tradition. Art as commodity is based on the assumption that a special individual is the originator and thus the owner of a work of art. This assumption does not recognize the collaborative process that produces art or the textuality of the author (Bennet 2005). In *BA*, the allusions to oral tradition deconstruct the idea of the romantic artist while suggesting that art can be a medium of exchange among individuals that can result in change among them. In the inner story, Alex and Iris discuss their relationship through the science fiction stories. They communicate their wishes and criticism with their suggestions for the plot. In this sense, the tale telling in the inner story, and Fevvers and Liz's tale telling in the first section of *NC* resemble each other. In both performance, art appears as a medium of exchange among individuals and is part of the relationship between the tale-teller and the listener. As it is in oral tradition, the time of tale-telling and receiving the tale are not separated.

In *BA*, the idea of collaborative writing and the uncertainty as to the originator is indicated first by the book Iris publishes under Laura's name—here, the ownership is not an easy matter to solve. Also, Iris points out to the spiritual presence of Laura in her writing process (626). Without Laura, Iris could not have produced the novel because Iris' identity is formed by reflecting herself on Laura. Laura becomes the double of Iris; the celestial artist and the banal individual body respectively. While Laura is idealized as a woman writer in literary circles, Iris becomes a nerve-racking hinder for critics with her perverse replies to their letters demanding information about Laura's life. In addition to the suspicion as to the author of the inner-story—which is at least confided in the reader—there is also doubt about the author of the stories in "The Blind Assassin." Although Iris imparts to us that it was herself who wrote the novel and it was she who had an affair with Alex, we have access to the nature of this affair only in the inner story, and in the frame story, Iris does not write about what they did in their secret meetings. She only says that she wrote the book as "a memorial" (626). Then, there is no evidence that it was Alex who told the stories; it can be Iris herself who wrote them.

Furthermore, the frame narrator's references to her daily activities like doing the laundry, the failings of her body, and eating subvert the idea of the artist as a genius or a prophet- the romantic artist. In

"Preface to Lyrical Ballads" which is accepted as the manifesto of the romantic poetry, Wordsworth explains that the poet is a specially gifted person who is a kind of slave to the operations of the mind although these operations are the result of deep meditations. The poet assumes a prophet-like status and art has a divine status. In *BA*, the mention of hands and pen mock the idea of the romantic artist who writes without a body, his art flowing out of him. The mention of the failing old hands brings the reality of the body into her art and thereby her art loses the spiritual, celestial quality. Iris frequently plays with the authority and reliability of the narrator by conveying the moment of writing, as follows for instance: "But on this page, a fresh, a clean page, I will cause the war to end—I alone, with a stroke of my black plastic pen" (93). For Iris or the woman writer, the act of writing means dealing with representations of her body and recognizing herself as a woman representing the silence end of discourse.

The intertextuality of the novel also puts the concept of the author in the center of the discussion of fiction since intertextuality reveals the novel as a text that is part of a general text, language, in which the author also becomes part of the language rather than the originator of art. In "Revolution in Poetic Language" Kristeva argues that each text is intertextual in the sense that each text is created by transposition of other texts. Intertextuality is more than allusions to other texts; she stresses that it is the "transposition of one (or several) sign-system(s) into another" (Kristeva 1980, 111).[11] The novel is a signifying system which has multiple meanings since it consists of various signifying systems, discourses. In this context, the author, too, becomes part of the signifying system that limits, structures, and produces the meaning and thereby texts lose the divine quality that romantic artists attributed to them. As Barthes argues in "The death of the Author," the author exists only in the text as an agent rather than the originator, guarantor of the text's meaning. Again, the idea that the writer is an effect of language appears and this position deprives the writer of his/her dominance over the text. The author then, in the intertextuality of writing relinquishes the divine position as the originator of a work of art.

---

[11] Kristeva does not only say that the novel is necessarily intertextual but she also says that language is always intertextual because of its nature.

The narrator's ironic use of invocation indicates the problematic position of the woman writer in literature. In *Negotiating with the Dead,* Atwood argues that writing is closely attached to death. In addition to the idea that writing is a resistance against death and mortality, it is also a trip to the world of the dead to get knowledge from that world. The world of the dead can also be the literary heritage from where the writer seeks help. In her invocation of the wolves and the dead, especially dead women, Iris expresses the difficulties for the woman writer to get help from the literary heritage. Her spirits, helpers in writing are the dead and deadly women like Medusa:

> Wolves, I invoke you! Dead women with azure hair and eyes like snake-filled pits, I summon you! Stand by me now, as we near the end! Guide my shaking arthritic fingers, my tacky black ballpoint pen; keep my leaking heart afloat for just a few more days [...] for haven't we been well-acquainted in the past? (607).

Instead of invoking the beautiful nymphs, muses as done in poems, Iris invokes the wolves, the frequent element of stories; the bad, dark side of the soul that exists in every being. This play with invocation also indicates a criticism of the male poet who derives his art from the image of woman by objectifying her in his art. The nymphs serve the male artist for whom woman is objectified in art as she is objectified in the formation of his identity as his other. The female does not have her own voice in his art; she is the object of desire that inspires him. The traditional invocation of nymphs erases woman as an active agent by incorporating the female in the male discourse; woman becomes the object of the male desire whereas the female desire is left in silence. When woman takes up the pen to write as a subject, she faces the difficulty to get help and inspiration from literary heritage: she is left with the frightening dead women, which is Iris' case. In her invocations together with her struggle with language, Iris explores what it means to write as a woman writer in language and literature in which the woman writer has to toil away with her situation as a woman. Since she finds herself as the object of the male discourse and the other of the male artists, she has to confront language in order to gain subjectivity.

In *BA*, the changing of seasons and vegetation as a result accompanies the narration. It gives the sense of time flowing, developing towards somewhere: flowers dying and growing again in the garden with the seasons changing. This suggests that the narration is developing to a point, too. Meanwhile, this effect of continuity of the cycle of end and beginning blurs the distinction between the end and the beginning since the death of Iris and thus the end of narration means Sabrina's return, which is announced in the papers after Iris' death and the publication of the *BA*, the book in our hands. The death of the narrator at the end of the novel is not actually her death then, but it is her birth since it is the novel in our hands—or in Sabrina's hands—that makes Iris exist as a narrator. For Iris to be present, a subject, she must vanish, that is, finish her writing so that she can exist as the narrator for the reader. Fiction is the absence of life for if Sabrina returned, Iris would have "no need for this jumbled mound of paper," instead, she would speak with Sabrina (637). Then, the presence of Sabrina would be the absence of fiction; the presence of the novel that is Iris' death is what makes her present. Reminding the reader of the condition of her existence as a narrator, Iris once more refers to the fictionality of the "I."

Unlike the ending of *NC, BA* does not offer marriage or a union with man, but there is death that will invoke life in the end. Atwood proposes to construct a different female subjectivity in language and in this sense, *BA* can be thought of as completing *NC* by experimenting with a new language that can place woman as subject (of her desire). Carter cannot get out of the literary tradition that prescribes marriage for the end of the novel, but seventeen years later, Atwood makes a bolder move by ending the novel with *a new woman,* Sabrina who will "reinvent" herself in language (627).

Thus, we have Iris' "trousseau" in our hands. Iris gives her trunk in which she puts her sufferings under the dominance of the male desire without *a language of her own* and her experiments with a new language to her readers who are addressed as Sabrina who is set free of the blood tie to the paternal line and as Myra on whose paternal hereditary she casts suspicion although they were never tied with blood to any men and male line has always been a suspicious matter since blood connects us to the mother only, not to the father. Hence, in her trousseau, Iris offers a different conception and construction of subjectivity in language that can cut the umbilical cord that still attaches the subject to the mother and feeds on her and can recognize the maternal ancestry that can guard peace and productivity in society, and give voice to female desire.

CHAPTER THREE

MORPHO EUGENIA:
NOSTALGIA AND HEAVEN

Nostalgia and Heaven

Like *NC* and *BA*, "Morpho Eugenia"[12] has got a dense
intertextuality and a woman writer, namely Matilda, as its protagonist who
at first appears as a minor character and turns out to be the heroine in the
life of the protagonist, Adamson. Despite resemblances that far, ME
differs from the other works mentioned in that in ME, the woman writer's
writing has the function of enlightening Adamson's life and serving his
interest. Both of the fairy-tales written by Matilda and the governess Miss
Mead provide clues to enlighten Adamson about his marriage with
Eugenia and thus they contribute to the construction of the male subject
and his knowledge. In addition to contributing to Adamson's
understanding of the circumstances in Bredely Hall, these fairy-tales
express Matilda and Miss Mead's restlessness about their powerless status
in the class system rather than the woman writer's anxiety with language
and her position within it. This shortcoming in constructing a female
subject and in focusing on female desire results from the employment of
deconstruction in ME that follows Derrida in using woman as a category
that destabilizes the definition of the (male) subject and truth without
attempting at constructing woman as the subject of her desire.

Byatt deconstructs identity and status in ME through analogy and
metaphor, and proposes that status and identity are not stable or natural
constructs since they are apt to change in the course of time and they gain
different significance and meaning depending on the angle they are
perceived from besides being constructed differently in different human
societies or animal communities. In addition to analogy and metaphor,

---

[12] It will be referred to as ME hereafter.

Byatt presents Adamson and Matilda who belong to neither the leisure class nor the middle class as in-betweens that vitiate the stability of status and meaning in order to deconstruct the idea of a natural or a rational order. However, the deconstruction in ME is in Derridean fashion and is not in accord with Irigaray's emphasis on the need to allow woman a subjective position, because Byatt does not give voice to female subjectivity, and suffices with demonstrating the artificiality of the idea of a stable identity.

While the use of metaphor and slippery analogy deconstructs identity and stable meanings, this deconstruction does not take into consideration sexual difference, which results in the absorption of the female subject in the male subject. By presenting class and status as the determining factor that establishes common interests among the characters or separates them, Byatt proposes class as the main source of power and means of domination. This preference for emphasizing class domination over articulating sexual difference reveals itself in the representation of woman, the relationships among women, and the lack of focus on the desire of/for the mother.

Adamson and Matilda are both difficult to situate in either the servant class or the leisure class while their lack of a profession to support themselves financially excludes them from the middle class as well. Matilda Crompton, the daughter of a tutor to bishops and landless like the other dependents in the household, lives with the family since her breeding and long-established way of life do not allow her to work. Similarly, William Adamson is also an in-between character who comes to the house as a sort of assistant to Harald Alabaster and depends on the family financially. Their status in the family is as he himself realizes "uncertain" which makes these people uncomfortable and excluded from the leisure-class family in the house (75).[13] Their exclusion from the family necessarily brings them closer to the servants but still they cannot be part of this group either and they need to be selective when they make friends among the group of servants. Matilda, for instance, chooses the company of Miss Mead, the governess, and keeps a certain distance with the other

---

[13] References to ME will be given as page numbers in parenthesis hereafter.

servants. These characters show that class distinctions and the boundaries between them are not static or clear-cut.

As a tool to criticize the social structure, Byatt sets a contrast between the Alabaster household, and the ant and bee colonies. Although Adamson finds analogy "a slippery tool," Byatt presents the analogy as a way to understand human society by emphasizing the strong resemblances between the social insects and the Alabaster family (100). Hansson argues that this analogy does not provide a steady meaning, but I contend that the differences between the ant colonies and the Alabaster household remain weakly expressed in contrast to the similarities that function as clues to reveal the nature of Adamson's marriage to Eugenia (Hansson 1999, 455). The emphasis on the similarities between the large ant queen in her chamber and Gertrude in her parlor are strong; both are fed by other females, the worker ants and the female servants, and the basic function of Gertrude and also Eugenia is represented as reproduction. The differences which are that Gertrude's servants include menservants as well and that Gertrude reproduces for the name Alabaster are not mentioned. Adamson perceives Gertrude as the center of power in the household. However, he does not realize that Gertrude exists and reproduces for the man who owns the women and children, and "sets all in motion" (76). Despite these differences, the order in the ant colonies, the status of drones, and the incest which is natural among the social insects give clues to Adamson and to the reader about what is going on in the house. At the end of the novella, it is revealed that Adamson is no more than a drone, and the children are the production of the incestuous relationship between Eugenia and Edgar, her half-brother. In this sense, Byatt presents the ant colonies as a reflection of the Alabaster household.

The metaphor of butterflies dominates the whole novella, which, like the analogy, discloses both similarities and differences. However, again like the analogy, this metaphor functions as a key to the message of the novella which is that change is part of life and appearances are misleading. Hansson argues that the differences between human beings and butterflies render this metaphor a tool that provides multiple meanings and it destabilizes overall conclusions; however, the fact that this metaphor reveals the hidden facts about the household makes it central in the novella (Hansson 1999, 462). This metaphor refers to the possibility of change as an ugly caterpillar transforms itself into a beautiful butterfly, and to the delusive appearances like the Death's-head Hawk, that takes Seth to his savior in Matilda's fairy-tale. Byatt emphasizes metaphor together with metamorphosis as the central concern in the debate on identity. Both of these words have the Greek word 'morpho'—shape—in them and suggest the idea of another thing; metaphor refers to something other than the said or written one and metamorphosis is the change into something else. When we combine them with the motto of Matilda's fairy-tale which is "things are not what they seem," universal truths and certain meaning evade for change makes stability impossible while form and meaning clash. The beautiful Eugenia like the *femme fatale* in Matilda's fairy-tale, becomes despicable in Adamson's eyes in the end; Matilda, the silent, modest, dependent woman is the creative, resourceful, intellectual woman that changes Adamson's life. With this metaphor, the gap, even clash between form, meaning, and names come to be the central theme in ME. Like Derrida, Byatt emphasizes "the *play* of the structure" and shows that meaning slips out of signifiers making the establishment of fixed meaning impossible (Derrida 2000, 90, italics in the original). In addition, this metaphor also deconstructs the idea of natural sex boundaries. With butterflies, it is the male that must be attractive to the female whereas in human society the females have to adorn themselves to attract males. Like the analogy, metaphor also functions as a tool to question a natural or rational order necessary for the continuation of life. In spite of the fact that there is no one-to-one correspondence between these communities, the central function of the analogy and the metaphor in terms of the resolution of the plot in ME renders them steady. With the metaphor of the butterfly Byatt points out the vulnerability of identity in a world in which change dominates life. Campbell argues that ME recounts the processes that change people and their life describing how Matilda and Adamson are transformed into liberal individuals during their study of ants (Campbell 2004, 158 -159). However, when it is considered that neither Adamson nor Matilda's sense of identity and their imaginary which includes how they relate to themselves and to the others or the other have not undergone a change, the change of Adamson and Matilda's life at the end of the novella does not signify the construction of a different subjectivity or relationship between man and woman. The setback in the way of change lies in the representation of woman and the repression of female desire in male dominated discourse that revolves around class hierarchy.

The solidarity among the servants and in-betweens, the powerless people, against the family members does not exist among the women and class comes to draw a sharp boundary between the lower-class women and the upper-class women. Adamson's isolation from the family leads him to Matilda's companionship and they form an alliance in the course of their study of ant colonies that turns out to be a study of their own status as well. The research team becomes a counter-power including the underprivileged members of the household, the children and the servants; however, the members of this research team are not on equal terms and there is hierarchy among them. Matilda and Adamson avoid informing the other servants of the publication of the book and this collaboration leads to the liberation of only Matilda and Adamson from the Alabasters, leaving the children and servants behind. On the other hand, Matilda has reservations about Adamson as well: she does not add her fairy-tale to the book for she means to publish her own. It is hopeful for the female subject that Matilda as a woman is aware of the fact that she still must keep her own resources to herself and protect her name on the cover of the book.

Yet, despite the hierarchy in this group, they act cooperatively against the family with a sense of belonging to the group of the powerless. This sense of belonging to the same class does not appear among the women. The women of the leisure class and servants have no concern for each other other than being rivals like Matilda and Eugenia, or Matilda and Miss Mead since Matilda leaves her behind with the family as well. Thus, Matilda's awareness of her difference as a woman from Adamson does not result in a change in her relationship with women. The fact that gender does not affect the principle that attaches the members of this counter-group to each other signifies that class and economic differences dominate sexual difference in ME. This means avoiding the fact that gender criss-crosses class distinctions and that women form a sort of class with common interests.

The representation of woman and the relationships among them in the novella is like a prescription for the representation of women for the perpetuation of patriarchal culture. Women are represented as if they are *content in their* object position, interested only in their physical appearance and competitive among themselves without threatening male power. The competition for power and for man is implied with the very structure of the plot. The novella opens and goes until the marriage like a fairy-tale: three beautiful daughters, a handsome man to choose among the sisters, and tests, duties to be completed before the young man can marry one of them. This fairy-tale structure presents suspicions as to the character of the sisters and implies that there are dangers awaiting the young man mostly due to both a secret knowledge kept from him and/or a flaw in his character that deludes him about the intention of the sisters.

Despite these resemblances, the continuity of the narration after the marriage breaks the structure of the fairy-tale: the handsome man, here, Adamson, wins the 'princess' who proves to be no princess in the end, but Byatt does not raise the question of what ideology governs this structure even though she disrupts the expectation from this genre. The three sisters are depicted as rivals, which is made obvious when Rowena receives an offer and Eugenia is anxious about getting married at the same time as her younger sister. The rivalry appears between Matilda and Eugenia as well. Matilda contrives a plot to expose Eugenia's relationship with her half-brother and takes her place as Adamson's partner in the end.

Rivalry among sisters appears in Miss Mead's fairy-tale, as well. In Miss Mead's fairy-tale, again, there are three sisters who are represented as jealous of each other. One of the sisters, Psyche, is married to Cupid and this marriage is destroyed by the curiosity of her sisters. It is also noteworthy that what brings bad fortune to Psyche is that she misses her family. Then, in this tale, the condition to have a happy marriage for a woman is to turn her back on her family and sisters. Again, in this fairy-tale, it is a man and marriage that is proposed as the cause of jealousy among the sisters. As the cause of this tension and competition among women, Byatt suggests a need for liberation from class domination and the desire for man -Matilda's for Adamson, for instance. On the other hand, Irigaray interprets this rivalry as the result of non-represented, unsymbolized desire for the mother. The relation to the mother is what Byatt does not represent in the novella apart from highlighting the breeding function of women. Thus, although Byatt deconstructs identity, she does not question how women are represented and why. The condition and ideology of representation is not represented, which makes any attempt to create an alternative subjectivity or society vain.

As it is obvious in Matilda's fairy-tale, the father-son relations dominate the representation in the novella and the mother-daughter relations are almost non-existent. Matilda and Adamson seem to have no mother at all. Matilda mentions about her father who was a tutor as the source of her intellectual character whereas there is not a word about her mother (118). Adamson, as it is apparent in his name, is the son of a father who was a Methodist butcher and his mother is not mentioned.

The family history of the Alabasters also highlights the father-son relations and the transmission of property and power from father to son. This family belongs to the leisure class who lives on others' labor, but their money comes from the middle class through the women married to the Alabaster men: Robert Alabaster's wife whose father was an East India merchant, then Harald's brother's wife, the daughter of a rich minor earl and Harald's wife, the granddaughter of a mine owner complete the noble but useless name of the Alabaster men with the money that they inherit from their fathers (22). The fact that in the nineteenth century the leisure class had already lost the economic structure on which it had depended before and became an anachronism makes it impossible for the Alabaster family to survive without aligning itself with the middle class that makes money by working. By way of marriage to moneyed women, the Alabaster men avoid the fate of the leisure class members who have to live as "hangers-on," because of their long-established aversion to labor in a society in which the landed-money had given way to the middle class (Veblen 1994). In this history of the family, women appear only as the provider of money and reproductive machines rather than being subjects.

In *The Theory of the Leisure Class,* Veblen argues that women become no more than property for the leisure class men by spending their time unproductively on the proper type of activities like embroidery, dancing, and reproduction. Women serve men who originally in the early stages of barbaric society depended on their labor and now in this society they help to prove the male's power to afford leisure. Throughout the novella, detailed descriptions of dresses occur as an emblem of leisure class women. Veblen says that the fact that these dresses with large skirts are not suitable to move in make these dresses perfectly serve as a proof that these women do not have to work for a living (Veblen 1994, 104). Women support men's sense of identity and status by proving that they spend their time conspicuously even when they are not visible to other people with proper leisure class activities, thereby they show that men can afford their leisurely activities.

This lack of representation of the mother-daughter relationship reflects on the representation of women and the relationship among them. The critical approach to the unproductive, parasitic leisure class does not differentiate between the male and female members and places the women in the family on the same status as the men. The women in the family are depicted as women who live to consume and reproduce children for the continuation of the family like ant queens. Gertrude speaks twice in the novella; first in the first page, she reminds Adamson of his duty to attend the dancing that aims at finding husbands and continues to compare Adamson's resources, strength, and height to her sons ending in admiration of his intellectual capacities (34). The second time she speaks—again to Adamson—is initiated by Matilda and she asks Adamson to help Matilda and the children in their research. The representation of Gertrude makes her no different from the queen ants or bees; a living being that exists only for reproduction. Irigaray states that "in the absence of valid representations of female sexuality, this womb merges with woman's sex as a whole" (Irigaray 2000, 419). Gertrude, the mother, and her daughters are represented as women who are rivals in the marriage commerce and their relationships are not even mentioned apart from their distance to each other in a competitive manner. It is relation to a man, that is the third term in Irigaray's words, that attaches these women to each other.

Besides the fairy-tale structure of the novella, which implies that there is rivalry among the sisters, the fact that the house that the sisters and the young man meet in is a Gothic one immediately reminds the reader of the gothic romances in which secret crimes and mysterious events await the ignorant hero. Though there does not come about a real danger to Adamson's life, the fact that his marriage results in disappointment and the revelation of the incestuous relationship between Edgar and his half-sister Eugenia prevents the novella from becoming a parody of gothic romance. Yet, the mystery that plays a central part in gothic novels turns out to be no mystery at all but a social fact that is never spoken about. Irigaray says that the incest taboo hides the underlying desire in patriarchal culture and it makes the exchange of women among men possible (*This Sex*, 170). Because woman does not enter the symbolic as a woman but as a mother, man does not give up the desire for the mother and seeks for satisfaction in woman-mothers. Then, the incestuous relationship between Edgar and Eugenia is not a shocking fact but it is a *normal* relationship between man and woman in patriarchal culture in which a sister cannot become a woman and, the relationship between men and women stands on the axis of mothering and satisfying men's desire for the mother. However, this *normal* relationship looks subversive, because, as Irigaray argues, incest has to remain in the realm of pretense for the rules governing the social relations and the symbolic cannot be put into the symbolic (*This Sex*, 192-193). Therefore, the relationship between Eugenia and Edgar is no more than the open interpretation of the law of patriarchal culture, which puts the order in jeopardy like male homosexuality. The incest taboo and prejudice against homosexuality veils the desire that structures the social order.

Although Eugenia is depicted as a willing party in this incestuous relationship, Edgar's aggressive character and Eugenia's speech to Adamson after Adamson learns about this relationship raise suspicion about Eugenia's feelings about Edgar. Edgar abuses the child-servant in the house and it is mentioned that he is especially interested in working-class women while avoiding the leisure class women. Taking into consideration Swinnerton's comment that Edgar finds the working-class women stronger, one can say that Edgar is in need of believing that he is strong and of making sure that everyone is convinced of his strength. He strives to prove his strength by his abuse of these women as he does so by his treatment of horses which are strong, too (106). His tendency to rape women makes one suspect whether he rapes Eugenia as well. Moreover, Eugenia implies that it is Edgar who forced her into this relationship:

> I would stop it – I *did* stop it – I wanted to be married, and good, and – like other people […]
>
> 'Only – we could not stop. I do not think – he-' she choked on Edgar's name, 'meant even to stop – he – he is – *strong* – […] (151, italics mine)

Her desperateness is also apparent in her argument with Edgar in the saddle- room. Adamson observes that she is "agitated, even tearful;" she appear[s] to be pleading" while Edgar walks away angrily (46). After her argument with Edgar, Eugenia confides in Adamson her wish to die and her feeling of isolation from the people around her (47). It is clear that Edgar treats Eugenia the same way he treats his expensive horse and Eugenia does not seem to have power to control him. Lackey drives attention to Amy's, the scullery-maid's yielding to Edgar's abuse and the similarity between Amy and Eugenia's response about Edgar. Like Amy who cannot accuse Edgar of raping her, Eugenia, too, protects Edgar even though she seems to be under Edgar's control (Lackey 2008, 137).

The negative representation of woman also appears in Matilda's fairy-tale titled "Things Are Not What They Seem." Her fairy-tale can be read as a rewriting of the life in the house. Like Seth in the fairy-tale, Adamson is deluded by a woman's, that is, Eugenia's white beauty and trapped in a house as a result. Through this fairy-tale, Matilda gives clues to Adamson about the secrets of his marriage and the character of Eugenia and herself. Seth is shipwrecked and in need of help like Adamson who does not even have proper clothes when he comes to a promising house that is ruled by a beautiful woman. Unfortunately, Seth and Adamson's hope of happiness prove to be vain when the woman turns out to be a *femme fatale*. In his desperate situation, Seth gets the help of small, seemingly insignificant ants and a fairy, Miss Muffet as Adamson gets help from the thin, silent Matilda. In this fairy-tale, Seth has to become the size of an ant and then learn to see things differently in order to escape. First, he must believe the ants and let the ants transform him into the same size as they are in order to escape from the house. Then he realizes that what he sees as dragons and snakes in the garden are only caterpillars that will change into butterflies. Thus, he goes through a process in which he learns the art of naming which is shaping reality in a different way. The appearances and names delude Seth throughout his journey, which can be regarded as the moral of the tale.

Adamson, too, has to learn to look differently and to name correctly. Adamson's name is relevant here: he is the son of Adam so he has the power to name: naming is creating, giving meaning and also it gives power to the namer, like the dragons in the Earthsea who have power over everything because they speak the secret ancient language and know the true names. In this fairy-tale, Mrs. Cottitoe Pan Demos is represented as a castrating *femme fatale* who threatens man's power through the food that she offers them in her house. It is significant that this feast consists of fruits and she lives close to nature and far away from society and this reminds one of Irigaray's remarks on the time when the mother-daughter relationship was not repressed (*Thinking*, 12). Mrs. Cottito Pan Demos belongs to a different social order that empowers woman and respects nature and it is in contrast with the one that Seth comes from. This order precedes the exchange of women, the establishment of patriarchal culture which is called the transition from nature to culture by Levi-Strauss (*This Sex* 171). Her complaint about men demonstrates men's rejection of her values: "'How ungrateful men are,' said the lady. 'They will not stay, whatever we give them, they will not rest, they will *sail* away'" (122). Men always want more or in Irigaray's words

> So men must kill to eat, must increase their domination of nature in order to live or to survive, must seek on the most distant stars what no longer exists here, must defend by any means the small patch of land they are exploiting here or over there. Men always go further, exploit further, seize more, without really knowing where they are going (*Thinking*, 5).

The social order that Seth comes from is dominated by the father-son relations and it is the father's advice not to eat before being offered that protects Seth from Mrs. Cottito Pan Demos' magic. Both Adamson and Seth are sent away by their father: Adamson is disinherited because he is an atheist and Seth, as the traditional youngest son, has to find a way to support himself financially because his father's plot was too small for three sons. Both are never satisfied though they do not know what they want. They want to go further, to be great without knowing how to do so. In their search, they come across and are deluded by women who look attractive but prove to be harmful. Like Eugenia, Mrs. Cottito Pan Demos deludes men, but they have more in common. Eugenia's opinion of nature is noteworthy in this context:

> How *lucky* I always feel to live just here, of all spots on the earth. To see the same flowers come out every spring in the meadows, and the same stream always running. I suppose it must seem a very *bounded* existence

to you, with your experience of the world. But my roots go so deep...
(30, italics in the original)

Adamson interrupts here to express his opinion of nature in the Amazons that contrasts the monotony of nature in England. For Eugenia the peaceful, monotonous nature is satisfactory, but Adamson admires the struggling, aggressive, deadly nature in the Amazons. He is fascinated by, for example, the tree called Sipo Matador that grows on another tree causing it to collapse in the end and thus destroying itself as well (30). What attracts him is the deadly, wild, unpredictable nature as opposed to the silence and peace in England's nature. This attraction reflects the conception of the aggressive male sexuality, while Eugenia's attachment to nature reflects her satisfaction with the harmony in nature. Seth escapes the *femme fatale* and travels to the fairy's cave on the back of a butterfly called Death's-head Hawk in order to ask for help. Although this fairy is mentioned to be a female by Miss Muffet, Seth thinks that the voice he hears in his dream is "neither male nor female" but a "sexless" being like Matilda (138; 105). Besides, the name of the herb, Moly, that this fairy gives Seth to undo Mrs. Cottito Pan Demos' magic is significant. The fact that this herb is the one that Odysseus gets from the god, Hermes, creates another problem as to the sex of this fairy. The implications of this symmetry between this fairy-tale and the life in the Alabaster household reveal again the problem of the representation of woman and articulation of sexual difference in the deconstruction in ME.

The other two genres, *bildungsroman,* the story of the education and formation of a young hero, here Adamson, and romantic poetry that are embedded in ME imply the problem of sexual difference in deconstruction as well. Being a Methodist butcher's son from middle-class populated part of England where success by labor has become the dominant value, Adamson means to be "a great man" though he does not know in what terms (9). His high-esteem leads him to keep his journals in a bank and almost the only thing he took from the ship is his journal for they are the "record[s] of the development of the mind and character of William Adamson" (9). In a *bildungsroman* like *Great Expectations,* the protagonist goes through a process at the end of which he becomes mature and is incorporated into social order with a proper marriage. Yet, Byatt disrupts the traditional bildungsroman structure. Adamson starts with a beneficial marriage to Eugenia but the marriage proves unsatisfactory for Adamson, and he escapes with Matilda to the Amazons to live with indigenous tribes. Therefore, it is not possible to say that Adamson integrates into the social order.

Moreover, Byatt deconstructs his authority by showing how he is deluded about Eugenia and the Alabaster family. Adamson is introduced into the novella and enters the Alabaster family as an intellectual and scientist who observes human society just as he does social insects. With this character, Byatt reflects the era of the nineteenth century that witnessed the shock of Darwin's *The Origin of Species*. The narrator gives voice to Adamson's point of view and gives his inner thoughts that reveal his double consciousness as when he compares humans and animals, or the tribal people and the English society with the objective distance of a scientist towards what he observes. For instance, when he is ashamed of his arousal when he is dancing with Eugenia, he observes that the aim of this dancing is exactly to bring about sexual attraction and finding a partner, and upon this observation, he continues to conclude that the dancing he took part in the Amazons is not different in terms of purpose (6 -7).

However, despite his confidence and belief in his intellectual capacity, it turns out that he has failed to see Eugenia and Matilda for what they are. He constructs Eugenia as an innocent woman, which means that she is ignorant of sexuality for Adamson, while she has a relationship with Edgar. Despite his low esteem of Matilda, she is the one that helps him understand the life in Bredely Hall. Pearce suggests that by showing how Adamson is deluded about what is going on in the house despite his sense of authority, while Matilda, whom he perceives as an inferior, corrects his point of view and directs him to the reality, Byatt deconstructs the authority of the male and his "master narrative" (Pearce 1999, 400). Adamson also resembles Irigaray's description of the lover of wisdom who takes philosophy as a mental exercise without achieving any impact on life and are "incapable of governing their life and who nevertheless issue words claiming to instruct us on the most everyday and the most sublime" (*The Way*, 3). Then, Adamson's education is completed when his authority is revealed to be imaginary. Byatt gives the female, Matilda, the intellectual capacity and power to understand society better than the male subject, Adamson. However, this power and knowledge aims at assisting him in his studies and ambitions rather than expressing the woman's own ambitions independent of the male subject. Therefore, despite the unusual and disruptive end of the education of the young hero, the end is still problematic in terms of the female subjectivity.

Byatt also unravels Adamson's knowledge and wisdom with the allusion to the romantic poet Wordsworth's "Resolution and Independence". When Harald is trying to convince Adamson to assist him with his studies and delay his plans for travel, Adamson thinks of Eugenia and *"[his] mind's eye* was occupied by a picture of Eugenia" (17, italics mine). Byatt implies that Adamson is blind to the circumstances because his imagination prevents him from realizing the true intentions of others. Imagination is an important term for Irigaray. She emphasizes imagination, or the imaginary stage in the individual psyche as the significant ground on which the symbolic organizes the subjects in the social order relegating the desire of/for the mother to silence although it is a constitutive element in the fantasy that governs the subjects (Whitford 1991, 53-56). The allusion to Wordsworth implies that Adamson's view of woman is constructed in his imagination. What he sees in Eugenia is the woman he has created after a long isolation in the Amazons and on the boat on the Pacific for the fulfillment of his needs and desire, not a real woman (17). For Adamson, Eugenia is not a subject that he wants to learn about; she fulfills the gap that he has always suffered from and he wishes her to satisfy his desire, which is doomed to be disappointed.

Adamson's construction of Eugenia as the woman who satisfies his desire for the mother necessarily creates the other woman who endangers his sense of being and power like the doctor/witch of the tribe in the Amazons who heals Adamson. This woman whom he talks about as "That filthy *hag* in whose house I cured *myself* of the fever" represents a woman who jeopardizes his sense of identity with her difference, the hole, or the lack of the phallus that he negates (13, italics in the original). The *femme fatale* in Matilda's fairy-tale is also in the same category as this elderly woman. Adamson cannot acknowledge this woman's power and knowledge since his sense of identity rejects woman autonomous entity or sexual difference. As a result of his dependence on the mother and his rejection of woman, he cannot get satisfaction in his marriage with

Eugenia and desires to go away although he wrote in his journal that he
would die without her, because what he really wants is not Eugenia (13).
The formation of the mind of this hero proves problematic in terms of his
attachment to the mother and his seeking satisfaction in women in order to
satisfy his desire that he does not acknowledge.

Besides Adamson's scientific observations on the Alabaster
family, his tendency to name, as when he names Eugenia 'Morpho
Eugenia,' which, according to Pearce, shows his desire to control, also
gives him a sense of authority, but since it turns out that he is mistaken by
appearances, his authority becomes an illusion (Pearce 1999, 403). Both
Harald and Adamson desire to name an insect by discovering in the
Amazons as a way to achieve greatness and immortality. Yet, as Pearce
mentions, the names Adamson gives to people show that his perception is
faulty. Morpho Eugenia will no longer be beautiful in his eyes when he
finds out the incest. This naming tendency reflects the newly developing
scientific atmosphere of the English society which started by Darwin's
book based on his observations of the animals and plants. By elaborating
on the desire to name and Adamson's failure in naming correctly, Byatt
throws a critical glance on colonialism which is, as Spivak states, an
important ingredient of the representation of the English in the nineteenth
century and the construction of identity for the English (Spivak 1999,
113). Byatt reflects the colonialist attitude with absorbing the 'other' in its
own cultural context through naming. Though not mentioned in the
novella, the plants and animals must already have names in the native
language of the tribal people, but the English people rename the plants and
animals so as to replace them into English culture. Another critical touch
on colonialism appears in the description of the different signification of
the same color in the Amazons and in England. In the Amazons,
Adamson's skin color is perceived to be white whereas in England "he
seemed sultry-skinned, with jaundice-gold mixed into sun-toasting" (3).
Byatt points out to the subjective and unstable construction of identity by
showing how the same color gains different significance and gives an
individual a different status in different societies. It is noteworthy that
Byatt uses color to classify roughly the characters as the power-holders
and the powerless in the novella; Adamson, Matilda, Amy and the tribal
people are dark or brownish whereas the Alabasters are described as white

as the name also suggests. In this grouping, dark color is used in very general terms for the colonized, which could have become an imperialist discourse if Byatt had not brought this color issue into play to suggest the construction of meaning. However, Byatt does not use sex to group individuals. Thus, the deconstruction of Adamson's authority and the power bestowed on Matilda does not lead to a female subjective identity.

Adamson's delusion includes his perception of Matilda as well. He remains in ignorance about her identity even though they conduct a research and share their observations of ant colonies and their opinion of society as well. Adamson's inability to see her as a woman leaves Adamson in the dark even about her religious views. This inability implies that Adamson perceives her from the family's point of view, for actually her comments on the animal communities and Greek civilization tells a lot about her opinions (81). Matilda lives quietly in the house, but this does not mean that she accepts her status happily or that she is "content in [her] station" (38). In spite of her modest appearance which is her "outdoor identity," she is proud to have had a good education, which immediately brings into mind the close link between learning and dissatisfaction with one's status. Even her neutral tone, as Adamson observes, creates suspicion as to her meaning. As she is a dependant, she has to secure her place in the household in order to survive, which is only possible by hiding her true feelings and character. It is also possible that her discretion as to her opinions and character is her weapon; Robbins points out that "characterlessness" slips out of interpretations and interference, and thus out of power (Robbins 2006, 17). Although her plain dresses and her silent existence in the house makes her seem insignificant, she has power over the family and Adamson as well. She serves Gertrude when, for example, she calls Adamson to Gertrude's parlor and expresses Gertrude's wish to make Adamson a sort of instructor to the children, which is actually Matilda's idea. She always finds a way to achieve her goals silently without showing any signs as for instance in her preparation for the journey. Matilda plays an important role in Adamson's life in the house and his divorce in the end; as Adamson puts it, she has "transfigured my [his] prospects" (94). She gives clues to him intelligently about the true character of Eugenia. As Pearce points out, although Adamson seems to be a hero in Matilda's life, Matilda's involvement in the writing of his book and in the discovery of Eugenia in bed with Edgar makes Matilda a heroine in his life (Pearce 1999, 407).

Adamson's duty ends with the destruction of the existing order, his marriage, and the dawn of a new one at the end with the help of Matilda and the servants. The message that directs Adamson to see the true relationship between Eugenia and Edgar comes through "a misunderstanding" "when the house decides" as Matilda states (155). "The house," here, refers to the servants. The messenger is unknown; however, it is obvious that the sender of the message is not one of the masters or mistresses. According to Robbins, by the role of the messenger, the servants have a chance to express their antagonism and wishes securely for they are only the conveyors of news, gossips, and opinions. Byatt gives the servants power to be the originator of the message. Robbins argues that the commonplace functions of servants in the novel such as the messenger, the stable lad, the messenger who calls Adamson home in ME, are important and these functions help the servants express the opinions other than dominant ones. The servants' opinions reveal the "ideological aspirations and disturbances" in society (Robbins 2006, 54). In this way, these functions allow the representation of the 'unrepresented' people, the powerless and the disadvantaged groups. Robbins states that servants appear at random moments that are critical in the plot starting from *The Odyssey.* The word "fate," in Greek *moira* derives from the word meaning "share" (Robbins 1986, 28). Robbins suggests that appearing at random moments that shape fate, servants allude to a lost time when community allotted individuals their share from the wealth of the community. Thus, the commonplace functions of servants express the voice of community or the force wanting their *fate.* In ME set in the nineteenth century, servants are silent in front of their masters, but the governess and the dependant, that is Matilda, takes the place of the servants. Though there is no random interference of them in the plot—if the wordplay in the game of anagram in which Matilda discloses her knowledge of the incestuous relationship is excepted—the message that calls Adamson to Eugenia's room when she is with Edgar shapes his fate. The servants or "the people in the house" break down the order in Bredely Hall (155). The rebellion that the servants and the in-betweens started without speaking against the family comes to a conclusion with the revelation of the incest. This rebellion can be thought of in a general context; that is the rebellion of the people, the community against the privileged class. Matilda's frequently expressed wish to address a large number of readers and the "we" she prefers as the narrative voice can be interpreted as her seeking for the interest of "the general public" to ally herself with (108; 93). Yet, the rebellion of the powerless fails when Matilda, as a woman becomes an assistant to the son of Adam and turns her back on the mother.

Despite the fact that Matilda is the initiator of and Adamson's partner in the research of the ant colonies besides being the contributor to the book that is published in Adamson's name, Adamson is the one who gains the financial benefits from the book. Like the women in the family who support the Alabaster family financially, Matilda helps Adamson to achieve his aims. After Adamson is enlightened about his wife and Edgar, he goes through another process/transformation in which he learns about Matilda. In her attic room, she has her own name, which is not Matty, but Matilda and her personality that she keeps from her visible life. Matilda's discussion of her plans with Adamson in her room reveals the failure in creating a female subjectivity despite Matilda's consciousness of how sex effects Adamson's perception. In this discussion, she tries to prove her *equality* to Adamson, that she can survive in the Amazons like Adamson and that she is strong (156 -157). More importantly, she states that she wants him to be happy (158). Considering Adamson's, the man's, happiness in contriving plans and conditioning her happiness based on Adamson's happiness shows that Matilda subjects herself and her desire to man's desire rather than living her own desire. Matilda then mimics the desire that is allotted to her in the male economy of representation, and this means that she fails to achieve a subjective identity despite her rebellious character. The scene in which Matilda turns out to be a 'woman' for Adamson and Adamson expresses his interest in her that he kept from acknowledging before is significant in that becoming a woman is indicated to be equivalent to desiring a man and replacing another woman, Eugenia. She gets rid of the "sexless" mask and becomes a woman with her passions and pursuits by undoing the plaits of her hair and shaking it: "And her face between the dark tresses was sharp and eager and hungry" (105; 157). Matilda's red shawl in the last scene on the ship again emphasizes her womanhood that is represented as attraction to man. The idea of change that is implied in the departure for the Amazons to start a new life like Adam and Eve fails to be convincing. Matilda's subjection to male desire and Adamson's construction of his identity and of woman upon his silent desire for the mother implies that this destruction of the order and deconstruction of identity does not produce an alternative or a positive statement about the production of a different subjectivity.

Byatt also elaborates on the fall of the leisure class and the continuity of the rise of the middle class. The duty of sorting out is significant in the novella. At first, it refers to Adamson's job in Bredely Hall. He starts to live with the Alabasters in order to sort out Harald's collection of dismembered insects that he keeps in the stable. Moreover, Harald wishes Adamson to help him prove his theories on religion. Harald works on a book which can prove the existence of God while embracing scientific methods and discussions as well. Adamson does not agree with Harald about nature and religion and therefore he cannot be of any help to prove Harald's theories. Harald's desperate ambition of making a convincing, rational argument to prove the existence of God is doomed to fail because Harald's belief in God stems from his inability to break his long-established way of life and beliefs. He is "too old" to accept the new world that is ruled by mutation, adaptation, and necessity. Moreover, his fruitless studies reflect his useless and aimless life style as a representative of the extinguishing leisure class. Melikoğlu states that it is the aristocratic greed to accumulate wealth without making any use of it that drives Harald to collect these pieces (Melikoğlu 1998, 41). His collection of insects is useless and his studies do not produce anything useful.

The argument of evolution and religion forms the background of the novella by creating the ground of conflict between the leisure class and the in-betweens. Adamson and Harald seem to have opposing opinions on this issue, however although Adamson is an atheist with scientific aspirations, his imaginary follows the patterns that are drawn by religion. What attracts him to the Amazons is the analogy he finds between the Amazons and "the Golden Age," "the innocent, the unfallen world, the virgin forest, the wild people [...] as our first parents" (30). Irigaray contends that this longing for the golden age, nostalgia for the past is the expression of the desire for the first home, the womb, or what she calls the maternal-feminine (*An Ethics*, 52 -54). For Irigaray the unacknowledged desire for the lost womb is the ground of the idea of God. Although Adamson and Harald differ in their approach to God and religion, they share the same imaginary that makes the idea of God possible. While Harald believes in the loving God, Adamson substitutes the Amazons for God and this expresses his desire to return to the mother (*An Ethics*, 59). The fact that rejecting the existence of God is not an easy matter is also expressed by Harald who cleverly sees the deep roots of religion in the social order and the connection of the God and the taboo of incest. He says that "the religious sense—in some form or another—is as much part of the history of the development of mankind as the knowledge of cooking food, or the taboo against incest" (34). Although his argument aims at proving the divine Intelligence, the existence of God, he hits the significance of the idea of God in the organization of gender relations and family relations. Lackey mentions another common problem of the mentality of Harald and Adamson, which is that Adamson is anthropomorphic in his observations on the social insects as Harald is in his conception of God as a projection of man (Lackey 2008, 132). Adamson realizes that "Our God is ourselves, we worship ourselves," yet, still, the male imaginary governs his ambitions and his search for liberation and greatness (103),.

In spite of the fact that Byatt deconstructs Adamson's perception and authority over knowledge, or his master narrative, and despite the intertextuality, the narration in ME is consistent. The novella demonstrates many aspects of the Victorian novel as well as Victorian issues. Yet, since it was written in 1992, the touches of postmodernism render the novella as Heidi Hansson calls a "hybrid of realism and postmodernism" that results in a fairy-tale-like story (Hansson 1999, 452). Again, as Hansson argues, the intertextuality does not provide multiple voices in the text, which reflects on the representation of woman. Moreover, unlike Carter and Atwood who use intertextuality as part of their aim to cross genre boundaries because these boundaries pose constrictions to female subjectivity, Byatt does not question how genre allies itself with gender. This is apparent in her use of fairy-tale structure where the sisters are represented as rivals in marriage commerce. While the genre boundaries are transgressed, the ideological ground of these genres or more specifically, sexual indifference dominates the novella.

The end of the novella leaves the reader with hope in Adamson and Matilda who, leaving behind the leisure class family, religion, and class barriers, set forth for a new world to start a new history for the humankind like Adam and Eve. The idea of change is again brought forth with the appearance of a butterfly brought by the captain Papagay, who is also golden-brown again. This butterfly conveys the idea that change awaits the escapees. This butterfly has strong wings but the wind can carry it a long distance. The wind here symbolizes both the environment and chance—carrying the implication of moira, fate—and it combines with individuality that is both intelligence and biology. Here again, Byatt achieves to destabilize easy explanations, fixed meanings, and clear definitions. However, although the two in-between characters' abandoning the family structure for a life in primitive societies and the idea of change that is implied by the metaphor of butterfly seem to indicate the birth of a new world in which class demarcations, religion, and family structure will not dominate human relations, I conclude that the journey that Matilda and Adamson set about cannot end anywhere much different from the one they escape from. Irigaray's observation that the idea of God has to be analysed in the frame of sexual difference explains the failure of Adamson and Matilda's project of creating difference in ME. Despite the optimistic end of the novella, Adamson and Matilda's future in the Amazons is bound with their relation to the origin, the mother which is still to be represented and explained. Byatt suggests a hope for a change in the social structure but there are setbacks in the way she creates the female subject since Matilda becomes a mother-woman to Adamson who does not recognize his mother just like her. The problems with the representation of woman in ME demonstrate that deconstruction cannot create a different discourse. It is not enough to deconstruct the authority of the male subject over knowledge since without acknowledging female desire, the desire of/for the mother, woman continues to occupy the ground on which the male constructs his subjectivity.

CONCLUSION

HOPE IN SALVATION THROUGH THE MEANS OF RUIN

Angela Carter tells the story of a female picaresque character, Fevvers, in search of a female subjective identity other than the idea of woman that is constituted in language and is in accord with the patriarchal social order in *NC* written in 1984. In this journey, Fevvers goes through the institutions that patriarchal culture has produced, and this travelling displays the possibilities, the roots, or the dangers they present to the female subject. In 1984, Carter knows that it is the language that a woman has to deal with in her quest which revolves around the conceptualization of the female body according to the male desire. Yet, as a woman writer, just like her protagonist, she stops short in hysteria as to how to be, how to write after abandoning the history of victims and the vain attempts of mimicry. Fevvers' hyteria and the disorderly situation she finds herself in at the end mirrors the woman writer's confusion about how to end the novel other than the traditional ending which is marriage and the maintenance of the order. The woman writer unites the lovers in the end though not in marriage, but this union preserves the potentials of hysteria to express female desire. *NC* ends at the dawn of a new language in the process of being written by man, Walser, and also the women comrades, Fevvers and Liz.

In 2000, Margaret Atwood, like Angela Carter, looks back at the history of women, the mothers, grandmothers, and also at the history of literature but unlike Carter, Atwood liberates her protagonist—writer, Iris from the boundaries of genre and gender. Besides rejecting the traditional end in marriage, she asks the reader to collaborate in the writing of a different language at the end of *BA*. Addressing the reader as Sabrina who has run away to India in order to avoid the sins and evils of the family institution, Atwood calls the reader into question and evokes her to join in giving voice to female desire. *BA* breaks free of the mimicry and hysteria of *NC* even if only to offer death for the end of the novel. Yet, death is not that separate from life; it brings life, Sabrina even though not in Iris' narration. *BA* does not only reveal the limits and constraints of language but it also breaks free of them through subversive moves like writing on writing, including the reader in the narration and turning the reader into a character, Sabrina, in the end. Atwood suggests that it is not only the woman writer's job to write a language that can produce female subjective identity but the (woman) reader has a responsibility to contribute to this process.

ME written in 1992 after *NC* and before *BA* presents a different case in that Byatt appears to pose an antifeminist stance as Hansson also mentions for the representation of woman and the relationships among them fit to the proper definition of woman in patriarchal culture (Hansson 1999, 461). Even though Byatt aims at deconstructing the natural or rational order in human society and the idea of stable class and gender identity, she fails to reflect what purpose these definitions serve to. This shortcoming prevents the change in language and social order that the novella aims at. When the change that Irigaray attempts to bring about in the here and now is deferred into future in the Amazons, hope loses ground. The easy and naïve expectation that escaping to faraway places with a desire for freedom which is such a complicated, many-faceted, and frequently a meaningless word that we shape according to our desire for power, rebellion, or love is not convincing. It is clear that the golden age that Adamson and Matilda take off for will neither gratify Adamson's desire for *greatness* nor Matilda's desire to *start living* when we take into consideration Irigaray's remarks that the nostalgia for a lost past is an impossible wish to return to the first house, the womb of the mother. Hence, Byatt places herself in the heritage of Derrida who thinks talking about woman as subject means to fall back on phallocentricism and suffices with deconstructing the male subject.

Even today, I believe that Irigaray's insistence on the need for a female subjective identity is still important since without producing a positive statement, or a concept of a subject that does not obey the law (of the phallus), deconstruction does not change the condition of woman either in language or in society. Therefore, making a difference, a change requires a female subjective identity as the producer of her own truth. Irigaray's argument for a different language that can represent the two sexes' desires and for a different subjectivity in order to release the subject—both woman and man—from the vicious circle of death and destruction (of the subject, God, desire, truth etc.) is important today when death and destruction is already the norm of our culture.

BIBLIOGRAPHY

Atwood, Margaret. 2001. *The Blind Assassin*. London: Virago Press.

Atwood, Margaret. 2002. *Negotiating with the Death: A Writer on Writing*. New York: Cambridge University Press.

Austen, Jane. 1994. *Pride and Prejudice*. London: Penguin Group.

Barthes, Roland. 2000. "The Death of the Author". *Modern Criticism and Theory,* edited by David Lodge with Nigel Wood. London: Longman.

Baudrillard, Jean. 2005. *Simulakrlar ve Simülasyon.* Translated by Oğuz Adanır. İstanbul: Doğu Batı.

Bennett, Andrew. 2005. *The Author.* New York: Routledge.

Boehm, Beth A.1995. "Feminist Metafiction and Androcentric Reading Strategies: Angela Carter's Restructured Reader in *Nights at the Circus*". *Critique*, Vol. 37, Issue 1.

Braidotti, Rosi. 1994. *Nomadic Subjects: Embodiment and Sexual Difference in Contemporary Feminist Theory.* New York: Colombia University Press.

Bouson, Brooks J. 2003. "'A Commemoration of Wounds Endured and Resented': Margaret Atwood's *The Blind Assassin* as Feminist Memoir". *Critique*, Vol. 44, No. 3.

Buchel, Michelle Nelmarie. 2003. *Bankrupt enchantments' and 'fraudulent magic': demythologizing in Angela Carter's The Bloody Chambers and Nights at the Circus.* Diss. University of Pretoria. (Online). http://upetd.up.ac.za/thesis/available/etd-10282004103512/ unrestricted/00dissertation.pdf

Burgess, Anthony. 1996. *A Clockwork Orange*. London: Penguin Books.

Bronte, Charlotte. 1994. *Jane Eyre*. London: Penguin Books.

Byatt, A. S. 1993. *Angels and Insects*. London: Vintage.

Campell, Jane. 2004. "Angels and Insects." *A. S. Byatt and the Heliotropic Imagination*. Waterloo: ON, CAN: Wilfrid Laurier University Press (Online). http://site.ebrary.com/lib/bahcehehir

Cella, Laurie J. C. 2004. "Narrative "Confidence Games": Framing the Blonde Spectacle in Gentlemen Prefer Blondes and Nights at the Circus." *Frontiers*, Vol. 25, No. 3.

Carter, Angela. 2001. *The Sadeian Woman and the Ideology of Pornography*. New York: Penguin Books.

Carter, Angela. 2003. *Nights at the Circus*. London: Vintage.

Curti, Lidia. 1998. *Female Stories Female Bodies: Narrative, Identity and Representation*. London: Macmillan Press Ltd.

De Beauvoir, Simon. 1993. *The Second Sex*. Ed. and Translated by H.M. Parshley. New York: Alfred A. Knopf.

Dancygier, Barbara. 2007. "Narrative Anchors and the Process of Story Construction: The Case of Margaret Atwood's *The Blind Assassin*." *Style*, Vol. 41, No.2 (Summer).

Defoe, Daniel. 1987. *Roxanna*. London: Penguin Books.

Derrida, Jacques. 1978. *Spurs: Nietzsche's Styles*. Chicago: The University of Chicago Press.

Derrida, Jacques. 2000. "Structure, Sign and Play in the Discourse of the Human Sciences." *Modern Criticism and Theory*, edited by David Lodge and Nigel Wood. Longman.

Derrida, Jacques. 1989. "Women in the Beehive: A Seminar with Jacques Derrida" *Men in Feminism*. Ed. Alice Jardine & Paul Smith. London: Routledge.

Dickens, Charles. 1980. *Great Expectations*. London: Penguin Books.

Fielding, Henry. 1999. *Tom Jones*. Hertfordshire: Wordsworth Editions Ltd.

Finney, Brian. 1998. "Tall Tales and Brief Lives: Angela Carter's Nights at the Circus." The Journal of Narrative Technique, Vol 28, No: 2 (Spring), 161- 185.

Forster, E.M. 1987. *Howards End*. Ed. Oliver Stallybrass. London: Penguin.

Hansson, Heidi. 1999. "The Double Voice of Metaphor: A. S. Byatt's 'Morpho Eugenia'". *Twentieth Century Literature*, Vol. 45.

Horn, Pamela. 1975. *The Rise and Fall of the Victorian Servant*. Dublin: Gill and Macmillan Ltd.

Homer. 1991. *The Odyssey*. Translated by E.V. Rieu. Penguin.

Irigaray, Luce. 2004. *An Ethics of Sexual Difference*. Translated by Carolyn Burke and Gillian C. Gill. London: Continuum.

Irigaray, Luce. 2000. "The Bodily Encounter with the Mother" *Modern Criticism and Theory, edited by* David Lodge and Nigel Wood. London: Longman.

Irigaray, Luce. 1985. *Speculum of the Other Woman.* Translated by Gillian C. Gill. New York: Cornell University Press.

Irigaray, Luce. 2004. *The Way of Love.* Translated by Heidi Bostic and Stephen Pluhacek. London: Continuum.

Irigaray, Luce. 1994. *Thinking the Difference: For a Peaceful Revolution.* Translated by Karin Montin. London: The Athlone Press.

Irigaray, Luce. 1985. *This Sex Which Is Not One.* Translated by Catherine Porter and Carolyn Burke. New York: Cornell University Press.

Kérchy, Anna. 2004. "Corporeal and Textual Performances as Ironic Confidence Trick in Angela Carter's Nights at the Circus". *The Anachronist*, Vol.10.

Kristeva, Julia. 1980. "Revolution in Poetic Language." *Desire in Language: A Semiotic Approach to Literature and Art*, edited by Leon S. Roudiez. New York: Colombia University Press.

Lacan, Jacques. 1982. *Feminine Sexuality*. Ed. Judith Mitchell and Jacqueline Rose. Translated by Jacqueline Rose. Macmillian Press.

Lackey, Michael. 2008. "A. S. Byatt's "Morpho Eugenia": Prolegomana to Any Future Theory." *College Literature*, Vol. 35.

Le Guin, Ursula K. 1993. *The Erthsea Quartet.* London: Penguin.

Lechte John. 1991. *Julia Kristeva.* London: Routledge.

Melikoğlu, Esra. 1998. ""Morpho Eugenia": Masters, and Servants and the People In between" *Litera*, Vol. 13.

Michael, Magali Cornier. 1994. "Angela Carter's "Nights at the Circus:" An Engaged Feminism via Subversive Postmodern Strategies." *Contemporary Literature*, Vol. 35, No. 3.

Munford, Rebecca. 2007. "'The Desecration of the Temple'; or, 'Sexuality as Terrorism'?: Angela Carter's (Post-)feminist Gothic Heroines." *Gothic Studies*, Vol. 9, Issue 2.

Pamuk, Orhan. 2001. *My Name is Red.* Translated by Erdağ M. Göknar. London: Faber and Faber.

Pearce Margaret. 1999. "Morpho Eugenia": Problems with the Male Gaze." *Critique*, Vol. 40, No. 4.

Requem for a Dream. 2001. Dir. Darren Aronofsky. Artisan Home Entertainment.

Robbins, William. 1986. *The Servant's Hand: English Fiction from Below*. New York: Columbia University Press.

Robins, Alan. 2006. "Alias Laura: Representations of the Past in Margaret Atwood's *The Blind Assassin*." *Modern Language Review*, Vol. 101.

Rose, Jacqueline. 1982. "Introduction." In *Feminine Sexuality*. London: Macmillian Press.

Rubinson, Gregory J. 2000. "'On the Beach of Elsewhere': Angela Carter's Moral Pornography and the Critique of Gender Archetypes" *Women's Studies*, Vol. 29.

Shakespeare, William. 1994. *Hamlet*. London: Penguin Popular Classics.

Spivak, Gayatri Chakravorty. 1999. *A Critique of Postcolonial Reason*. London: Harvard University Press.

The Book of the Thousand and One Night. 1986. Translated by J. C. Mardrus. Boston; Routledge & Kegan Paul.

Veblen, Thorstein. 1994. *The Theory of the Leisure Class*. London: Dover Publications Inc.

Whitford, Margaret. 1991. *Luce Irigaray: Philosophy in the Feminine*. London: Routledge.

Wordsworth, William. 1993. "Resolution and Independence" *The Norton Anthology: English Literature*. Sixth Edition Volume 2. W.W. Norton & Company, Inc.

Yurttaş, Hatice. 2017a. "Desire in *Middlemarch*." *Languages, Culture, and Gender,* edited by Züleyha Çetiner-Öktem, Begüm Tuğlu and Erkin Kıryaman. İzmir: Ege University Press.

Yurttaş, Hatice. 2017b. "Reading "The Penelopiad" through Irigaray: Rewriting Female Subjectivity". Hacettepe University Journal of Faculty of Letters, Vol 34, No: 1.

INDEX